PRAISE FOR
THE PRICE OF SURVIVAL: MARCUS LEVIN,
NORWEGIAN HOLOCAUST HUMANITARIAN

"As much as we have continued to learn about the details of the Holocaust in past decades, there remain dimensions of the tragedy that are only now emerging into larger awareness. Irene Berman, in this her latest work, offers a moving and compelling personal account of the impact of the Nazi machine on the Jews of her native Norway. The courageous and untiring devotion of her father Marcus Levin to the salvation and well-being of the victims is a shining beacon in an era of fearful darkness. *The Price of Survival* is not only a loving daughter's tribute to her humanitarian father, but also a work of deep honor to the victims and hope to those who face unfathomable evil." —**Rabbi Jim Rosen**, Beth El Temple, West Hartford, CT

"Irene Levin Berman and her family have distinguished themselves in service and dedication to Norway for more than 100 years. Author, businesswoman, Ibsen translator for American theater, and activist, Irene has been on a mission to educate future generations. Many Norwegian Americans like myself are deeply grateful for her trilogy of three books that provide us with knowledge of our heritage. Our conversations over many years have enriched my understanding of my own Norwegian family. Her writing is powerful and compelling for all ages. This third book, *The Price of Survival,* continues the story of Norway and the Holocaust that has been virtually unknown in the United States." —**Karin Arentzen Stahl**, author of *The Option*

"Irene Levin Berman's newest book *The Price of Survival: Marcus Levin, Norwegian Holocaust Humanitarian* continues her remarkable history of Jews in Norway, this time adding many little known details about life there for those who survived the Holocaust. Told through her family's experiences escaping and returning after World War II, we learn of Norway's unwillingness to help resettle refugees in Norway after the war. The book shows the importance of one individual, Ms. Berman's father Marcus Levin, who helped returning Jews finding new lives with the help of the Joint Distribution Committee, International. After the war Mr. Levin was awarded the Gold Order of Merit by King Haakon of Norway. Anyone interested in the history of World War II and its aftermath will be grateful to Ms. Berman for sharing this compelling and intimate story." —**Peggy Shapiro**, retired associate director, Career Services, University of Connecticut School of Law

"In *The Price of Survival: Marcus Levin, Norwegian Holocaust Humanitarian,* Norwegian/Jewish author Irene Berman has accomplished two incredible feats: First, her tribute to the legacy of her father, Marcus Levin, which lives on for survivors and for her and her family today; and second her fascinating and chilling indictment of the war horrors perpetuated in Germany and Norway. No matter the issue, Marcus Levin's caring and compassionate presence was there. He aided in getting as many Norwegian Jews as possible to Sweden before the majority were sent to the camps to be massacred. All through the war and after his force and energy helped survivors through statelessness, housing shortages, and finding work. His focus on the children, including his own, was incredible. The most important event in his life was his association with the JDC—the Joint Distribution Committee. Together they helped expand his humanitarian work. He was admired everywhere, even receiving the Norwegian Gold Medal of Honor from the king of Norway to recognize and thank him for his work. Read about his take on unfairness, the difference between guilt vs responsibility, and the incompetence of the Norwegian Social Department. The entire Berman family must be so proud of his legacy and how he made a difference in the world." —**Roberta Prescott**, president, The Prescott Group

The Price of Survival
Marcus Levin, Norwegian Holocaust Humanitarian

Irene Levin Berman

HAMILTON BOOKS
Lanham • Boulder • New York • London

Published by Hamilton Books
An imprint of The Rowman & Littlefield Publishing Group, Inc.
4501 Forbes Boulevard, Suite 200, Lanham, Maryland 20706
www.rowman.com

6 Tinworth Street, London SE11 5AL, United Kingdom

British Library Cataloguing in Publication Information Available

Library of Congress Control Number: 2019933272

ISBN: 978-0-7618-7129-3 (pbk.: alk, paper)
ISBN: 978-0-7618-7130-9 (electronic)

∞™ The paper used in this publication meets the minimum requirements of American
National Standard for Information Sciences—Permanence of Paper for Printed Library
Materials, ANSI/NISO Z39.48-1992.

Printed in the United States of America

I dedicate this book to the memory of
my mother and father and what they gave me,
which has always stayed with me.
I have always loved the country of Norway which was
separate, but equal to being Jewish.
I am extremely grateful for my adult life with
my husband and my children in the United States.
I am fortunate to have three identities.

When the Lights went out on Norway
We fought, we tried, but we lost
The enemy fought, they brought Evil, they won
We saw them take our friends away
God wept, we wept
Three among eight hundred
Their Angels ran out of time
We saw them disappear into Darkness
We waved good-bye
God wept, we wept
The journey brought them to Evil
God wept, we wept
Yet Evil prevailed and destroyed them
God lost, we lost
Norway's darkest chapter
Among Six million lives extinguished in a bonfire of Evil
God wept and made us pray
We cried, we prayed and looked to the stars
God heard us and we will pray together
For eternity

Contents

List of Illustrations ix

Personal Introduction xi

Preface xiii

Acknowledgments xv

Why This Story? 1

1900: Beginning of a New Century 3

The Levin Family 7

Father's Life in Oslo 9

Pre-War Years 11

April 9, 1940: War 15

1941: The War Continues 19

October–November 1942: Germans Pursue the Jews 21

October 24–November 1942: Escape to Sweden 23

November 25–26, 1942: Escape and Arrest of Jewish
    Women and Children 25

The *Donau*—The Death Ship 29

The Extermination of Jews in Auschwitz 31

Efforts to Save Lives 33

1942–1946: Working in Sweden 35

Refugees and the Joint Distribution Committee 39

The War Is Over—Back to Norway 41

1947: Father's Philosophy—Personal Unresolved Issues 43

1945: Returning from the Holocaust 45

Return from Auschwitz: Post-war Contact with the Norwegian
Government in London 47

1946: Displaced Persons 49

1948: The European Children's Camp in Norway 53

1938: A Jewish Children's Home in Oslo—Boys and Girls
from Vienna 57

1953–1955: Minus Refugees 59

Circa 1960: Reconstruction in Norway after the War 61

Compensation for Norwegians 63

The King of Norway and the Watch 65

1965: Father's Last Years 67

Our Family Becomes Part of the JDC 69

1943–1946: Childhood Memories of Sweden 73

Learning about the Meaning of the Holocaust 77

Growing up Both Norwegian and Jewish 79

Looking Back with Ruth 83

January 2012: The Prime Minister of Norway Apologizes to the
Norwegian Jews 87

My Philosophy Connected to Prime Minister Stoltenberg 89

Afterword 91

About the Author 95

Illustrations

Leib and Henriette Levin   4

Marcus Levin   5

The Levin Family   9

Marcus Levin, Leif Arild and Irene   10

German soldiers on the day of invasion April 9, 1940   16

Jews on the dock before the departure of the *S.S. Donau*   30

Irene and Leif Arild in Sweden with new boat hats   34

Looking forward to a new life in Norway   50

Marcus Levin welcomes Golda Meier, former Prime Minister of Israel   54

Marcus Levin and colleagues greeting refugees   60

Marcus Levin receiving the Norwegian Medal of Honor   65

Marcus and Rosa   66

JDC Conference in New York, including Marcus Levin and Charlie Jordan   70

Mildred Guttermann celebrating with three generations in Geilo, Norway   75

Irene and family in the United States   80

Aunt Makka, Ruth, and Irene   84

Personal Introduction

It is a great honor to write a greeting in the book of the Great Humanist Marcus Levin.

My family on my Father's side immigrated to Norway in 1912. My Mother A"H was a survivor of Auschwitz. She lost most of her family and was liberated to Sweden in April 1945 and married in Oslo 1947. Like most other Jewish families in Oslo the Norwegian holocaust had caused great losses, my Father A'H had lost his Mother, sister, sister in law, nephews and nieces. I grew up in Oslo in the 1950s and 60s and experienced many of the same feelings and deprivations that Irene so eloquently has described in this and previous books. For twenty years after the War, Marcus Levin and his work for the refugees in Norway, was an institution within the Jewish Community. It was clear to most that Marcus Levin took upon himself the almost impossible task to find housing for hundreds of refugees, who all wished to live in the capital close to the Jewish institutions. Norway after the War was in disarray and housing even for their own citizens was scarce. In addition came the social work needed to integrate refugees that in many cases were broken both physically and mentally. This impossible task did not deter Marcus Levin from taking up the fight.

On a personal note: I moved from Norway to Denmark in 1971 and in 1976 married Anette Guttermann, granddaughter of Alf Levin, Marcus's brother. Thus Irene became kind of a cousin. Many years after we moved to the U.S. in 1985 our paths crossed and we discovered how close our Jewish/Norwegian bonds were. In addition, through the Jewish community and the Synagogue in Oslo I had close ties to many of Irene's family members both on the Levin and Selikowitz side.

This book is a testament to the work of Marcus Levin and Irene is thereby fulfilling the Mitzva of Kibud Av v'Em, honoring one's parents. May you be merited with a long life.

Howard Ganz
Lawrence, New York
January 1, 2019

Preface

This is the story of Marcus Levin, my father. Father passed away in 1965. He had dedicated every moment of his adult life helping the victims of WW2, before, during and afterwards. The older I got, the more I realized what an exceptional humanitarian he was. As a child I always took my parents for granted. I always expected them to be present when needed, as natural as night and day, each in their own way.

Terms like *Holocaust* or *Shoa*, the Hebrew term, were totally unheard of when I was a very little girl. Gradually I came across words like *war, fighting, fiends*, and *bad people*. Oh yes, and the term *Jews*, became well known.

When I became inspired to write about Father's unique life, I realized how much I had actually remembered. The idea for this book awakened only a few months ago when I came across a document on my computer ignored and forgotten for at least a year or perhaps longer.

Coincidentally I received a letter from Bjarte Bruland, sent to me jointly with my brother Leif Levin. Together they had prepared a twelve-page document consisting of Father's history from the onset of WWII, until he passed away in 1965. Although I remember the various events characterizing him as a humanitarian, I never really understood the significance. Bjarte and Leif's documents caused me to reflect further. Little by little, years of memories suddenly came to mind like it was yesterday, for which I thank them.

Bjarte Bruland was always proactive in supporting Jews who he had always respected. While studying at the university, he got increasingly more involved. He had heard about father and that he unfortunately passed away in 1965. Bjarte read everything he could get his hands on. He introduced himself to my brother, Leif Arild Levin.

The two men decided to read through all possible documents jointly as well as any other important information planning to learn as much as possible about

Father. Thereafter Bjarte ended up as an expert on all kinds of major and minor details referring to the Holocaust and has published several books about the same topic.

Leif concentrated on all of Father's activities as well, including sharing his personal memories. This provided some unknown information, rendered by Leif and me, allowing us to find even more unexpected information yet to come.

This thirteen-page document describes most of the documents which father had left behind in his office. I had naturally heard of father's strong, yet independent approach based on leaving nothing behind. His energy was spent finding ways to make it possible for the few surviving stateless Jews to survive. I considered myself extremely grateful to have received all the details, passing their work on to me, now living in the USA.

I will never forget how Bjarte and Leif helped make it possible to bring my childhood's memory back, here in the USA.

Acknowledgments

I want to thank Eleanor White, my good friend and editor. And I thank Joanne Kurnik for her incredible patience, help, encouragement, and skills.

I would also like to thank the JDC for use of one photo. The rest of the photos are from the Levin family collection.

Why This Story?

The first time I was given the opportunity to speak about Norway and WWII in the United States, I raised the following question: "Who has heard about the attack of Jews in Denmark by Germany?" Most people had heard about it, although only a few were really familiar with the history. However, when asking the same question about the history of Norway, most Americans were totally unfamiliar with the circumstances.

There was a specific reason why I wanted to write this story. I found that most Americans, regardless of background and religion, were uninformed about the horror occurring in Norway. Why? Because the country was small? Maybe. Unknown?

It took me several years to realize that Norway was indeed the smallest country in Europe, in view of the number of Jews living there. But I also realized that Norwegian Jews had the highest percentage of persons killed, with only a similar degree as Holland, which was attacked a few months after Norway.

Knowing that most Americans are unfamiliar with what happened in Norway during the World War II, I'll start here by providing a brief background.

As most of my readers know, Adolf Hitler rose to power in Germany in the 1930s and he decided that all Jews should be annihilated, forcing everyone around to support him. He insisted that Jews were central to an enormous world conspiracy aiming to destroy Germany and the German race. His entire view of the world became affected by this totally insane belief. He was responsible for the deaths of about six million Jews, as well as another five million disabled people, psychiatric patients, homosexuals, Romani, political prisoners, and others in the concentration camps.

Vidkun Quisling, a minister's son, was born in July 1887 in Telemark, Norway. Initially he helped needy men in the Soviet Union and thereafter collaborated with Norwegian hero Fridjof Nansen around 1920. In 1931 he was ap-

1

pointed as the first secretary of defense, helping two governing groups involved with various agricultural activities (Norwegian Bondeparties). Thereafter he quickly involved himself in fascism. In 1933 he formed a group that was referred to as the Nasjonal Samling (also known as the NS, meaning "National Union" and allied with the Nazis) and was appointed the leader of the group. The Nasjonal Samling never reached a political breakthrough and had no representative in the Parliament. From 1936 the party was considered a private group. Simultaneously, anti-Semitism became increasingly more popular both with Quisling as well as among the general membership. Quisling felt that Norway had been affected negatively by the Jewish influence.

In December 1939 Quisling met with Adolf Hitler on several occasions in Berlin. In April 1940 Quisling warned against Great Britain and felt that Germany ought to invade Norway. At the same time Quisling attempted a coup d'etat broadcast over the radio, but Hitler appointed a German named Joseph Terboven as senior official in Norway. In September 1940 the Nasjonal Samling became Norway's sole allowed political group, and by 1942 Quisling was officially installed as the head of the government, with the title Prime Minister.

Quisling was always seriously anti-Semitic, whether he was speaking in person or writing, regardless of the issue. In the fall of 1940 he, his government, the Nasjonal Samling, and the police worked nonstop to complete the deportation of all the Jews in Norway. While some Jews were smuggled out of the country by the Norwegian resistance, more than 700 Jews died in the concentration camps during the Holocaust and only a small number of those who were deported survived the camps and returned to Norway.

Once the war came to an end Quisling was tried, condemned to death, and executed on October 24, 1945. During the formal trial, he agreed that he was indeed anti-Semitic, but he claimed that he did not realize that the Jews were being deported. Quisling's name is now commonly used to indicate that someone is a collaborator or traitor.

1900
Beginning of a New Century

Father was born in Christiania, the capital of Norway (the name was changed to Oslo in 1922), in 1899. He was one of nine siblings; the fifth child of Leib and Henriette Levin. When he passed away in the next century, Jewish life in Oslo had gone through enormous changes, having been exposed to a catastrophe of incredible dimensions.

Father was just a couple of years old when his family moved to Rjukan which was a small but active industrial city where many newcomers settled. Occasionally the area was also inhabited by transient Jews, but the Levin family remained for many years. Leib Levin, our grandfather, eventually realized it would be impossible for his children to maintain a Jewish identity without an active Jewish environment. Therefore, the family moved back to Christiania in 1918 where Leib Levin opened his own store. By then father was eighteen.

A few years ago I came across an article in a Jewish magazine referring to a speech delivered by Leib Levin on May 17, 1914, the hundred-year anniversary of the original introduction of the constitution on May 17, 1814. In 1918, Leib was involved in the local business world. He was an active and popular Jew.

The local council selected Leib as the speaker when the special anniversary took place. He explained the changes which had allowed Jews to become Norwegian citizens. Henrik Wergeland had encouraged the people to stand by the changes more than 50 years earlier. The latter was the most beloved poet in the country who devoted his energy, intellect and intense feelings to convince Norwegians to alter the original laws forbidding Jews from settling on their soil. The new law had been passed on May 17, 1852, finally allowing Jews to live in Norway. Jewish people had already been living in Denmark and Sweden for several hundred years. Grandfather moved to Norway around 1878.

3

Leib and Henriette Levin

Sadly, Henrik Wergeland passed away just a few years earlier, deprived of experiencing the change. In his speech, Leib Levin expressed gratitude and admiration in memory of Henrik Wergeland and his delivery was very well received. He praised Norwegians and the major change in the initiation of the constitution. He encouraged the newly-arrived Jews in Norway to be decent, fair, honest, and to avoid any problems and disputes. At the very end grandfather delivered a statement which came directly from his heart.

It is possible to live the life of a religious Jew, while simultaneously pursuing life as an honest and proud Norwegian. (The English translation, less fluid than in Norwegian)

This motto has remained throughout the country from that date until today. In retrospect, however, it is difficult for me personally to realize how many non-Jewish people ignored the Jews, although many of the latter who suffered might have benefitted from more sympathy.

Leib was one of the few newly-arrived immigrants who encouraged other Jews to move to Norway once the change in the constitution took place. His attitude was totally positive and he decided to learn the native language as quickly as possible.

When he first arrived prior to his marriage, he stayed in the Northern part of the country working hard to make a living. On the 10th of April in 1889 he applied for Norwegian citizenship which was immediately accepted. I still have a copy of his official paper. Thereafter Leib once again moved back to Oslo where he befriended a group of other Jewish men. A private Jewish organization was established where members could pursue their own religion. He then made a trip to Sweden looking for a Jewish wife as, or so he was told, there were no single young female Jews in the country. He soon met Henriette Kransdorf from Gothenburg, Sweden who he fell for immediately and asked for her hand in marriage. She came from a large family and was seriously concerned whether she wanted to move to another country. However, the way we heard it told by our grandmother many years ago, she was so impressed by the young man that she accepted his offer. Their marriage took place in Sweden, and they subsequently moved to Norway, an "unknown" country.

Marcus Levin

The Levin Family

As time went by the family experienced the end of the nineteenth century, welcoming the twentieth. Despite Leib Levin's experience in Rjukan, he was convinced that it was the right decision to move back to Christiania (Oslo) as his children got older and would benefit from growing up with other Jewish youngsters.

Father and his siblings were active in the Jewish Youth Community in Oslo. Although the Jewish Men's Group was limited, an active organizational life flourished particularly centered around the Jewish Youth Community. Father was an enthusiastic member, especially when they started organizing annual summer camps for Jewish children. This was originally intended as a counter plan against a local mission attempting to convert destitute Jews to Christianity by offering them summer vacations. To avoid the missionaries' plan, the Jewish Youth Community collected enough funds to support summer camps, as well as a home for Jewish children without parents. In 1932 a summer house for the children was also made available in the country. Father became the leader of the Jewish Youth Community and later the trainer for the organization's gymnastic group.

Father's Life in Oslo

In 1930 father acquired a store in Oslo and in 1933 he married Rosa Selikowitz. Leif Arild was born in 1935 followed by my birth, their daughter Irene, in 1938.

As mentioned, my brother's name is Leif Arild. Initially my parents had decided to name their first born after Leib Levin who passed away only a few

The Levin Family

months earlier. The family story is as follows: Telegrams were sent to all their relatives and friends announcing the arrival of the newborn baby. They soon received a variety of greetings from friends congratulating them on the birth of Leif, one of the most popular boy's names in Norway. My parents were smart enough to leave the Norwegian spelling, realizing it would be best for their child. I feel strongly that grandfather would have been equally pleased had he known his name was carried on by his grandson in the Norwegian version!

Marcus Levin, Leif Arild, and Irene

Pre-War Years

Horror occurred all over the world. As bad as it seemed initially, no one ever realized the catastrophic events that were to disrupt humanity.

Father was involved with the Jewish Relief Organization which became of great importance to him. This group had started in Christiania in 1906, and was aimed primarily towards destitute Jews in the capital and other parts of the country. After the Russian revolution and the massacre of Jews in Ukraine and Poland, the organization began to seek funding for Jewish assistance in these areas. It wasn't until 1930 or so that the organization really became active in helping the Jews and Father automatically helped people who needed money.

With Hitler empowered in Germany in 1933, the political and Jewish refugees started to escape from various countries. Acquiring permission to move from their own countries to other countries was difficult—even impossible. Norway was one of the few countries that had very strict asylum conditions, and through political research it has become evident that these conditions were discriminating against the Jews. The criminologist Per Ole Johansen wrote about the Norwegian refugee politics in 1938 as follows:

> Levin's early organizational experience played an active role when he started work-ing with refugees. His particular involvement with these types of problems remained until the time of his death. There is no doubt that the serious situation in Germany from 1933 and subsequently thereafter with the increase of anti-Semitism must have played a significant part. Just as significant was the equally important Jewish belief which consisted of doing something good for other people, as well as also making sure to take care of their own. In diaspora the Jews developed a special social man-ner of thinking which consisted of the same philosophy. Levin had been raised in exactly this tradition.

However, Father focused on one issue only which consumed all his time. He felt that most of the Norwegian Jews had ignored the immigrants and felt strongly that this important work must have been misunderstood. Those in charge of this work—initially a businessman, D. Goldberg—had full respect and admiration for the efforts provided for the refugees. But they were virtually alone. Father's goal was to hopefully change the human mentality.

Kristallnacht (German) (Referred to as the Night of Broken Glass), was a pogrom against Jews throughout Nazi Germany on November 9-10, 1938, carried out by military forces and German civilians. It created yet another enormous shock around Europe.

In 1938 the American Jewish Joint Distribution Committee (also known as the JDC) began to play a part in the Norwegian-Jewish efforts to help the refugees. The JDC was established in the United States in 1914 to help Jews in Eastern Europe and Russia from suffering due to war activities which had generated a highly acute humanitarian need. The organization was actually a form of a distribution organization—a joint agreement among several American Jewish organizations. From 1933 to 1939 the organization participated in helping 375,000 Jews out of Germany and incorporated areas—a significant achievement against serious odds.

During the same year the Jewish Relief Organization in Norway changed its name to the Jewish Help Organization; a name which was more in keeping with the spirit of the time. Many Jews made a tremendous effort to help the Jewish refugees who came to the country. Among them was Elias Feinberg, the leader of the Jewish Help Organization. He was Father's mentor as a social worker. Another person was Herman Valner, Father's brother-in-law. Valner was a prominent businessman in Oslo. The government demanded a financial guarantee in the amount of 5,000 kroner for each refugee comparable to a standard annual salary at that time. Until 1940 Valner provided financial aid for more than twenty refugees. Both Valner and Feinberg were subsequently deported to Auschwitz and killed.

I realize most of the names I have included in the last few sentences may not be familiar to most, but these men were referred to many times by my parents with emotion, respect and sadness. Some of them were also my relatives, and although I cannot remember them, I still have occasional contact with their children and grandchildren.

Only a few Jewish refugees could be helped in Norway due to the extremely strict refugee policy. However, Norway could be used as a transit country for refugees who expected to obtain a visa to a country overseas. Most of the Jewish refugees in Norway had a temporary permit to stay but no permit to work. In the fall of 1939 the Jewish Help Organization, together with other organizations such as the *Nansen Aid (Hjelp) Organization*, was responsible for providing funds for housing and food for close to 300 Jewish refugees.

All together 350–400 refugees succeeded in reaching Norway when Germany attacked in 1940. Most of them were virtually stateless having been deprived of their countries when they left German, Austrian and Czech soil. Those who managed to escape to Sweden when the Norwegian Jews were targeted in 1942 would once again experience a difficult set of problems when returning to Norway after the war.

The Help Organization was run by Odd Nansen, another Norwegian humanitarian with whom Father worked. One of their goals was to help refugees leave the Central countries where the Nazis initiated attacking the Jews. Nansen was the son of the famous polar explorer Fridtjof Nansen, the 1942 Nobel Peace Prize winner.

While working with refugees, Nansen was arrested and first sent to prison in Northern Norway and thereafter to Auschwitz. Because Nansen was not a Jew, he was kept in a different section. He suffered terribly as well, but managed to survive in another camp which was located far from his Jewish friends.

While imprisoned, Odd Nansen left a hidden message in his camp. I assume his purpose was to ensure that the treatment of Jews should become known eventually, in the event he was annihilated before the war came to an end. His paper reads as follows:

> All the Germans without exception are Jew-haters and treat them worse than animals. No one will have any scruples about hitting them or satisfying their sadistic tendencies by plaguing and torturing them in order.

In the meantime, the Jewish Help Organization had been forced by the Gestapo to take over all the social responsibility connected to the Jewish refugees in Norway demanding that the Jews should not become a burden on the Norwegian state. This resulted in a greater burden on the organization. A monetary collection was organized by the Jews throughout the country as a special social taxation from the Jewish congregations in Oslo and Trondheim. Norwegian Jews loyally participated in handling this taxation and it was quite unusual to experience any problems with collection. Some Jews also contributed significant additional funds for this social work.

April 9, 1940
War

Germany invaded Norway and Denmark on April 9, 1940. The Danes surrendered immediately while the Norwegians fought a war of resistance. After intense fighting, King Haakon the Seventh escaped to London setting up a government in exile. People were apprehensive with no understanding as to what was awaiting the country. Bombing and shooting immediately took place. My brother Leif was five when the war broke out and I was two. I don't remember that year, although Leif observed both foreign planes near our house and air alarms.

Father became concerned, realizing the enormous and rapid expansion of the Germans throughout Europe. Several countries decided to remain neutral: Switzerland, Portugal, Ireland, Spain, the Vatican, as well as Sweden. The latter cooperated with Germany, allowing trains with soldiers to pass through on their way to Norway, aimed at increasing the German force. Having said that, it should also be noted that many Norwegian soldiers who had been in trouble with the Nazis and the Gestapo, were forced to escape to survive. They were immediately welcomed at the Swedish border. In addition, all the Jews from Norway quickly recognized the need to escape to Sweden as soon as possible to avoid German arrest. Sweden welcomed them and saved their lives.

Millions of Jews were killed in tragic ways. Norway was the smallest of all the European countries to be attacked. In 1940 when Germany attacked Norway, they had already registered 2,000 Jews.

Close to 40 percent of the Jews were deported from Norway and murdered in Auschwitz by the end of 1942/early 1943, once they were considered as no longer being strong and willing enough to work. Only strength allowed them to stay alive.

Those who managed to escape either reached Sweden or in a few instances England, but the large number of Jews didn't start escaping until the end of 1941–1942. Among the 2,000 registered Jews in Norway, 500 had come from

German soldiers on the day of invasion April 9, 1940

other countries in the nineteen thirties hoping for a safer environment, and to avoid the horror of the Gestapo. In order to leave their native countries they had to surrender their rights as citizens of the former country.

Immediately after the invasion on April 9 rumors spread all over Oslo. People were extremely concerned, wondering what would come next. On the following day most of the people anticipated bombing and other types of dangerous attacks. The most concerned were parents with children. My mother immediately decided that we should go to the mountains where we had friends, but she didn't expect Father to agree so quickly. She had anticipated that he would be reluctant considering all the other local concerns she knew he worried about. But Father had an additional plan for joining Mother, our housekeeper Ruth, Leif and me. We drove for many hours until we reached Fagernes, a place in Valdres, located in the Norwegian mountains.

Father had made a close friend when he was in the military service several years before. The friend had already called insisting that the entire family should come to stay at his large farm. My brother Leif still remembers all the different animals. I remember virtually nothing except for seeing a big horse for the first time. Our family was very grateful.

The next surprise came early the following morning. Father explained that as his family was fortunate in having been welcomed to such a safe and generous environment, he felt obligated to participate in the defense of his country. That was where he felt he belonged. Father volunteered to serve in both the Norwegian as well as local forces and participated in violent battles near Bagn. When the Norwegian forces had to surrender, he was taken a prisoner of war. Primarily due to his knowledge of the German language, he was forced to function as a liaison between the prisoners and the German forces. After a relatively short imprisonment, the Germans released him and Father returned to Oslo with his family where he continued running his business.

1941
The War Continues

In 1941 the war was still ongoing. There was an acute shortage of food; schools were partially closed due to the arrests of resisting teachers; as well as shortage of heating and electricity as the fall weather began.

In addition to the ongoing fighting within the country, gradually it became known that Hitler's agenda was to seek out all the local Jews in addition to the stateless refugees in order to eliminate them.

The first war years consisted of an increase in anti-Jewish politics. It wasn't until January 1942 that an increased and systematic registration of the country's Jews was carried out by the German police together with the Norwegian police, which at that time was run by Nazis and pro-Germans. The horror increased and the remaining Norwegian Jews worried that something even worse would occur. However, the Jews couldn't even imagine the massive, widespread catastrophe they were to face.

After the war when Father had escaped to Sweden, he compiled a report regarding the occupational circumstances that occurred in Norway, when he, among other things, also described the various details that actually took place beginning in September 1942.

However, the actual full attack occurred on Yom Kippur, the holiest of all Jewish holidays. All Jewish private homes and apartments were seized by the Gestapo and two very well-known Jews were arrested while attending the service. The people now felt something horrendous was about to happen and anxiety prevailed. Most people still figured that the Gestapo would liquidate the Jews one by one accusing them of having broken the law. This opinion was also shared by actively involved non-Jewish Norwegians. However, they were wrong.

By the middle of 1942–early 1943, almost 800 Jewish men, women and children were deported and the annihilation in Auschwitz began. Only thirty-eight men survived when the war had come to an end. Approximately 1200 persons, 60 percent of the remaining 2000 Jews, escaped the country and survived.

October–November 1942
Germans Pursue the Jews

I have no memory of October 1942. Around the second week of October my brother Leif however remembers opening the door to our apartment when the doorbell rang. Two tall men dressed in suits, overcoats and hats asked for my mother who was just behind Leif. She made him go inside while she remained at the door. She had a suspicion as to who they were and what they wanted, but she played along letting them start. Without introducing themselves, they immediately asked for Mr. Marcus Levin. Mother remained calm, responding that he wasn't at home. When asked where he could be reached, she just said she didn't know. She continued that her husband was on a business trip looking for merchandise to be used in his store, which was hard to find those days. They hesitated for a couple of minutes and finally left.

Mother closed the door, telling Ruth about the conversation. Ruth had already prepared several packages of food for Father early that morning before he left with his brother Alf to go into hiding where they would wait for Norwegian resistance people who hopefully would bring them across the border. He left more than a month before us and had already escaped to Sweden by the time we left at the end of November. We did not see Father again until we all met in Sweden a month later on November 28, 1942.

Once he was settled in Stockholm, Father had to face the reality that he was the only surviving member of the hard-working core of the Jewish Center which had worked tirelessly to help other people escape.

As mentioned, Mother and the rest of us remained in Oslo until November 25. That particular day is my very first conscious memory of my life. I was at the park early on that day where Ruth and my brother came to pick me up from the playground where I was playing with my friends and teachers. It was around three o'clock in the afternoon. We walked back to the apartment where Mother was waiting. On the way Ruth told me we were going to *"the country to pick potatoes.* " The image of potatoes must have been very important because I can still remember discussing it with Ruth. Leif, walking next to us, said nothing. He didn't mention potatoes. Ruth had decided that it would be better for me to focus on a trip to the country looking for potatoes to keep me from asking when and how we would reach Sweden.

Mother was waiting for us at home. A very short time later we all left—Mother, Ruth, Leif and I. And yes, my cousin Frank came with us. He was the young boy of thirteen whose story is told later in this book. I do remember specifically having to leave my dolls behind. I know that my brother talked about lack of food on the way so he must have been quite hungry. I was told he talked intermittently about schools closing and darkness at night as it was illegal to light the streets. Where was my father? I also wonder how much my brother Leif, only eight years old, must have wondered and worried.

I assume Mother must have told me Father was on vacation, or away on business, as his lack of presence didn't seem to have bothered me. We left our home around five o'clock in the evening as it was getting dark.

October 24–November 1942
Escape to Sweden

Why did Father have to leave so quickly?

Two of father's brothers, Leonard and Sigurd Levin, had been arrested earlier than the majority of men and were incarcerated in the Northern part of Norway and at Grini prison. A month later they were sent on a separate ship to Auschwitz where they both died.

Sometimes just before the Gestapo State Police ordered the arrest of the remaining male Jews on October 26, 1942, Father went into hiding with his third brother, Alf Levin, and two of Mother's brothers, Arnold Selikowitz and Heiman Selikowitz. They hid in an empty apartment belonging to relatives who had already left. For several weeks they stayed in this apartment in total silence. Mother brought them food every night after dark.

Several weeks later they were contacted by a representative of the Norwegian resistance group promising to help them escape across the border. At the appropriate time, the four men were instructed by two Norwegian resistance men to hide in two separate locked armoires—two brothers in each cabinet. They managed to fit in the reasonably large pieces of furniture, which were carried down the stairs and out of the building. To prevent curiosity generated by the noise created by the heavy transport moving from floor to floor, the men carrying the furniture made a point of speaking in loud voices to each other. "Why do we need to transport these horrendous pieces over to the Nazis? Why couldn't they just pick them up on their own?" These remarks discouraged the curious onlookers who were afraid of getting involved or perhaps of being exposed to a Nazi who might show up.

When the armoires finally reached the street, a large milk truck was ready to bring them along the dangerous road to Sweden. Unfortunately, half way there the milk truck broke down. Miraculously both the drivers located an urban milk truck and the two armoires were moved. Fortunately no soldiers stopped to check on the milk truck's content. They finally reached the wide path in the woods which brought them to the Swedish border and safety.

Father seldom spoke about his war experiences but this was one he frequently mentioned. Among other things, he told us that when crossed the border, they heard the resistance people arguing. Both drivers insisting that the other was supposed to be responsible for the key, which was never found. Father heard them from inside the armoire and screamed as loud as he could, "Please break the damn lock and let us out."

The four men spent a peaceful night at a nearby bed-and-breakfast. The next day they dispersed to various areas according to the plan. A few years ago, I found father's receipt for that overnight stay which I still keep among my precious papers. When father left for Stockholm the next morning there was a job waiting for him with the Jewish Congregation Center where he worked continually while in Sweden.

November 25–26
Escape and Arrest of Jewish Women and Children

The women in my family were alerted to escape no later than November 25. The rumors spread quickly from family to family indicating that the next day, the 26th of November, the Germans planned a mass arrest of all the remaining Jews. Our small family consisted of Mother, Leif, me and Ruth, our long-time housekeeper. As mentioned, Father had already successfully gone into hiding, and was subsequently brought to freedom in Sweden. He actually had left at the very beginning of October only a couple of weeks prior to the arrest of the men.

Ruth Simensen, who I called Ruthin, had been our housekeeper since 1939. She was aware of all the work carried out by the Norwegian resistance as well as other illegal activities prior to the family's escape. The men in the resistance group were in and out of the house on a daily basis. When the family made plans to escape, Ruth was alerted that if she remained, she would most likely be arrested and exposed to torture. Based on this, she decided to escape with us.

Most of the Jewish women had remained in Norway, while so many of the men had been arrested earlier. Obviously no one had the vaguest idea how much more horror was awaiting them, and they worried about the men. The women were afraid to escape so soon after, fearing that the rage by the Germans would backfire on the incarcerated men. My father had alerted Mother that she should wait for a specific group of resistance people who had promised to bring us across to Sweden as soon as they could manage. In retrospect it is clear that my father was acutely aware of the horror that lay ahead, probably because of what he had already experienced.

Many of the employees at the Police Department remained in their previous positions even though the power was now in the hands of the Nazis. It was difficult to understand why they remained considering all the difficulties threatening the citizens.

Some of the women intentionally remained there as well to keep track of the plans to relay to the Jews. One of them was a close friend of ours. Around September 1942 Mother was told that serious events might take place soon. In November she heard that a large German ship was getting prepared to transport Norwegian Jews out of the country.

On November 24 my aunt Makka (Amalie), who was married to Bernhard Goldberg, heard from a friend that women and children were potentially in trouble and encouraged them to pack and hide. Makka spent as much time as she possibly could going from house to house warning as many women as possible.

Mother, who was ready to have the same resistance people take us to Sweden as Father, alerted her mother and three sisters, making certain they were all prepared to escape within three days.

Her mother and two sisters left on November 23. Her youngest sister Lotta (Charlotte) and thirteen-year-old son, Frank, were scheduled to leave on November 24. At that point Mother was convinced she had done what she felt was necessary, making plans to leave with her family on November 25.

However, Mother was in for a surprise. Lotta and her son had just left that very afternoon with Mother and her group ready to leave the next day. Or so she thought. Late in the evening she heard a knock on the door and to her surprise found Frank standing there crying. He explained to his aunt that he and his mother left in a car with two drivers and four Jewish women. The drivers took them to a railroad station two hours away where they were supposed to leave the car and continue on the train. Once they arrived at the platform the drivers noticed a fairly large group of German soldiers waiting for the train. At this point the drivers advised them to separate into groups of two to avoid suspicion among the soldiers. Frank got out of the car by himself and boarded the nearest train which to his surprise left immediately, but in the opposite direction—back to Oslo. Once he realized his mistake he panicked but remained quiet. The second the train arrived he jumped off and ran nonstop to our apartment. He felt that was the only solution.

Mother was naturally in shock after hearing the story and told Frank that he would join her group the next day. Therefore, our group now consisted of my mother, Leif (age seven), me, Irene (age four), Ruth, our housekeeper, and Frank.

As planned, we left the house at five o'clock in the evening in a very casual, yet quiet manner. Mother had been told by the same resistance people not to share her plans with anybody because there was always the chance that someone in the house might hear about it and inform the Nazis. Ruth and I walked down the back stairs of the building, while Mother, Leif and Frank went down the elevator. A resistance person waited for us on the street. We walked to a parallel street where a car was waiting for us so no one would notice anything unusual.

Once we were in the car the driver immediately stated that our lives were in jeopardy but they would do their best to lead us to safety. Fortunately, we were not stopped by any soldiers on the way, which was a great fear. We were able to board a train just like the group did the previous day. Ruth with her blond hair entered the train with Leif and me while Mother went alone, locking herself in the lavatory. Frank was accompanied by a resistance person who personally made certain that he was aboard the train. Luckily there were no soldiers on the platform.

A few hours later, we left the train and picked up by another resistance driver. He took us by car to a large farm. Around midnight, the owners helped our family locate the way to a hidden path which somewhat facilitated passage through the woods. At the age of four I was getting tired and was put in a large rucksack on the back of one of the resistance people. The rest of the group started walking on the path through the woods toward Sweden.

Mother mentioned to the two guides that she had heard that the ship *The Donau* supposedly was scheduled to leave the following morning, which was now, or perhaps only a few hours away.

I was told I slept the entire time while both Leif and Frank walked quietly with Mother and Ruth. Occasionally the two resistance people alerted them to speak quietly in the event there were soldiers in the area. Finally around five o'clock in the morning a yellow sign indicating Sweden appeared on a tree. Quickly we contacted the Swedish army which was standing by. Before we were given a chance to cross the border, guards demanded names and passports. Mother was the designated leader who presented our passports.

As we were allowed to cross the border a few minutes later an unexpected person in uniform appeared and said, "Do you have the boy?"

My aunt was naturally extremely distraught when she realized her son was missing as she was rushed to leave the car and board the train. She searched everywhere around the railroad station. Despite not finding him, she was forced to continue. The group boarded the train and moved on. When my aunt reached the border she was desperate, hoping against hope her son had been able to reach my mother. The family was reunited and Frank and his mother went to a small city in Sweden where his father was waiting for them. My father was in Stockholm waiting for us. There had been horrible chaos, with large groups of people being arrested while some had succeeded to escape to Sweden. The Swedish organization was flooded with letters and requests, and definitely needed help organizing the difficult circumstances.

In retrospect, I realize that I never heard the story about Frank and I often wondered how my aunt managed and if she profusely prayed that her son had enough common sense to return to mother's house.

Did she immediately think that he had decided to run to his aunt when the wrong train had brought him back to the Oslo railroad station? I remember that my aunt had always told him to go to my mother if he ever got lost! I didn't even learn of the reality of this bizarre story until the end of the nineteenth century.

Actually, everything that had to do with the war, the arrests and the terrible experiences, were kept from me and Leif. From what I have heard, this was the case with most of the children until sometime in the nineteen seventies. Parents were known to not discuss anything with their kids. They would lower their voices when a child entered the room. I moved to the United States at the beginning of the nineteen sixties and my life changed forever. Of course I remained in close contact with my parents as long as I could, but unfortunately they both passed away only a few years later. I often wish I had more time to talk to them as an adult, but that didn't happen.

After my parents passed away my relatives were wonderful and supportive and I spent much time with them. All my close relatives were focused on getting to know my small children whenever they came to visit. Obviously we all used this time to recover from the loss of family members.

Once in Sweden my parents rented a small apartment for the four of us and Ruth. In retrospect, only a few years ago, I realized that on the same date and hour we crossed the border to Sweden, 200 taxis were dispatched in Oslo to all the homes where Jews were still living. The Nazis had prepared a list of the remaining Jewish women and children, forcing them down to the docks to be deported on the ship the *Donau.*

The *Donau*
The Death Ship

On November 26, 1942 an enormous German freighter ship named the *Donau* sailed off from Oslo with approximately 585 adults and children. The ship's journey took about one week due to bad weather. Women and children of all ages were crowded together from top to bottom all over the ship. None of the women and children ever returned to Norway. The ship stopped in Stettin where the people were taken ashore, and forced to enter a number of freight cars where they were all tightly packed together, with no food. The train stopped at Auschwitz where they were separated according to gender, age and strength. Elderly and sick men, women and children were immediately sent off to a specific building where the end of their lives took place within a few hours. The men who appeared to be strong enough were brought in behind the well-known entrance to Auschwitz where they were put to work as long as they had the strength. Thereafter they were annihilated. Three more ships were sent in the same manner from October 1942 until January 1943. All together only thirty-eight men who were arrested in Norway survived the concentration camps in Germany.

Jews on the dock before the departure of the S.S. Donau

The Extermination of Jews in Auschwitz

I already mentioned the attack by Germany on Norway and Denmark which took place on April 9, 1940. The initial planning of deportation and annihilation was carefully scheduled around September/October 1942. This continued until January 1943 when German soldiers claimed they had located all the remaining Jews. The fourth ship loaded with Jewish prisoners, including my aunt and two cousins, left for Auschwitz at the end of January 1943.

A few years ago I realized that in late 1942 and early 1943 the Germans had learned to accelerate their already overloaded primary goal, consisting of quick destruction of millions of Jews who were obliterated in gas chambers. But it seemed they wanted more production once they had learned about a totally new idea. This particular system consisted of a special gas named Cyclone B. This gas increased the speed of annihilation. Consequently a larger number of victims were killed in the shortest amount of time. Initially I found this incredible, but discovered several articles confirming the same information. It was, and still is, hard to allow these thoughts to pass through my mind. Norway with their 2,000 Jews was among the very first European countries to be attacked. When the war came to an end, only thirty-five to thirty-eight Jewish men survived. Seven hundred and seventy Jews were killed around that time. I found it hard to look at pictures of Father's sister and her two teenage children.

This group included one aunt, two uncles, two young cousins and two uncles-in law from Father's family, as well as one cousin and one aunt from Mother's family. Why? How?

Efforts to Save Lives

My family's escape to Sweden was not organized through one of the large resistance groups but through a smaller group. They demanded a significant amount of money—approximately 40,000 kroner per trip in addition to incidental expenses—to help the family cross the border. When we all had arrived and were safe, Father paid what they demanded. However, little by little he gradually experienced mixed feelings about the monetary expenses. Reluctantly he considered the compensation for driving to be excessive under the circumstances. Subsequently he contacted the Norwegian embassy in Stockholm in January 1943. There was no doubt that the organization and its leaders had brought his family to safety—that was obviously most important, he said. Nevertheless, Father expressed bitterness in a letter stating that the group and their leaders hardly had operated with a patriotic initiative. It appeared they were primarily focused on a significant short-term monetary income. It wasn't the amount of money he reacted to; he would gladly have paid whatever was necessary. However, he felt the extra funds could and should have been utilized to help other people with fewer funds enabling them to escape as well.

I never heard about this issue until long after Father passed away. One of the people at the Jewish Congregation came across a copy of Father's letter pertaining to the group and its leader. I was told that Father had misgivings when he submitted the letter to the Norwegian embassy keeping track of many various issues while in Sweden. The more I think of him in this ethical situation the more I can clearly envision him. It must have been painful to send such a negative letter to someone else just after he and his family's lives had been saved. As time passed, however, I no longer think he could have done anything differently. The manner in which he expressed his disappointment was exactly what he as an honorable person would do. I am so proud of his action.

Father was immediately given a position at the Refugee Office located at the Jewish Congregation in Stockholm. Our family remained in Stockholm for four years. From late 1942 until 1946 father worked solely with refugee matters; both as a social worker as well as on refugee issues related to the Norwegian embassy and the government in London.

Irene and Leif Arild in Sweden with new boat hats

1942–1946
Working in Sweden

In May 1943 Father compiled a list of deported Jews in addition to those who were still under arrest in Norway. Father had already acquired some information about the deported Jews. However, signed postcards by prisoners in Auschwitz were addressed to friends and relatives in Norway. These postcards, a part of the SS plan, were aimed at fooling the world to believe that the Jews' destiny was different than the reality. The postcards provided an unreal description of their arrival in a bogus place. The horrendous destiny was concealed, to say the least. In his report Father wrote that he assumed the male Jews had been sent to a work camp in upper Schlesien (Germany) while women and children were interned in another place. The report however did not provide much attention from the Norwegian authorities in Stockholm or London. Nevertheless, Father still made a comprehensive, consistent record of everything until the very end of 1946.

The first and most important task which Father initiated was registration of all Jews who had been deported from Norway or those who were still imprisoned in Norway. He was also able to print forms which were distributed to those who had managed to escape from Norway. They were asked for a list of family and friends who had been deported or still remained in Norway. In this manner he was able to create an applicable index. This list was subsequently sent to the Swedish foreign department which used the information to put pressure on the German authorities regarding deported Jews with no connection to Sweden.

He also compiled a comprehensive overview of the Jewish men who had been left in the concentration camps in Berg outside of Oslo. Some of the Jewish women were kept at Grini, another well-known concentration camp outside of Oslo. These were the Jews who, according to the Nazis' interpretation, had so-called mixed marriages; in other words, Jewish men and women who were married to non-Jews, according to the Nazi definition of Jew. These individuals were,

35

for the time being, excused from deportation to Germany in accordance with the order from Eichmann's office at Reichssicherhelitshauptamt (sic) in Berlin.

By the beginning of 1945, many believed the German security police might change their opinion and consider deporting these Jews as well. Father realized early on how exposed this group was and personally made certain that the Swedish authorities were informed. The Swedish foreign department tried to get these Jews out of Norway. The authorities were not convinced if that was necessary, until just before the very end of the war. At that point Father once again had to play another key role.

The agreement which resulted in transfer of the Jews was negotiated by the leader of the Swedish criminal police, Harry Soedermann, when he visited Oslo late in April 1945. This took place just before Germany surrendered, which was not official. The main reason he came to Norway was to negotiate interim arrangements to get Germany to surrender to Norway. Regardless of differences in opinion with other Jews, it was important to get the full-blood Jewish people out to avoid being sent off to Auschwitz. The so-called level of security in being married to a non-Jew might not remain. Despite all the promises from the Germans, Father and others didn't trust their messages. Finally, the parties made secret arrangements. Fifty-two Jews were to be brought over the border by train to Sweden on May 2, 1945 for their safety. A list of the Jews, with a stamp provided by the German border guard, was found among Father's papers. Most of the fifty-two people who were involved with the transport had been interned in camp Berg since their arrest in 1942. One of the prisoners later wrote a description about the transport to Sweden which gives an impression about how dramatic it was for the prisoners once they had been told in the morning of May 1 that they were going to be moved.

Before the remaining prisoners were sent to Sweden, they were kept in local concentration camps, worrying about the unknown. They were naturally anxious about what might come next. Rumors spread everywhere. Some felt they were about to be sent to Germany, others felt they were to be moved to other camps. The optimists felt they were to be sent home, and some thought they might go to Sweden. The optimism dropped below the zero point when the ambulance from Berg Hospital drove into the camp with one of their prisoner friends. They were certain that he, because of the indifference on the part of the camp leadership, was doomed to die because he had been sent to the hospital too late to get competent medical treatment. Here is a comment which one of the men reported later:

> Therefore all of us believed that we were to be sent to Germany when they could bring such a patient back to the camp. We were given orders to place our luggage on the back of the truck. Naturally there wasn't adequate room for all of the bags for the forty-six men, so the remainder was left on the ground where the guard lost no time helping himself. We were all told to stand in three rows, in a stand up attention.

The person who headed the camp, Major Wallstad, who was feared, approached us with his hair hanging way down his face. He was so drunk that he could hardly stand. He gathered all the guards around him, and as I (sic) stood just behind them in the first row, I heard all that was said. His statement was as follows, 'Guys, it is not my fault that things are working out in this manner. It is the damn Red Cross. But we had to follow our leader Quisling to the very last moment. If it had been up to me, guys, you know what I would have done with them. Look at them. Shoot them down. And I will be responsible.' An acute feeling of horror went through me, but as I was quite depressed and weak after a prison stay of more than thirty-one months, I did not realize how dangerous this moment could have been.

Fortunately it turned out better. The remaining refugees still kept at the concentration camp in a place close to Oslo, ended up being sent to Sweden. Father felt strongly that they could not trust the Germans who had insisted that nothing would take place as they were planning to settle the war. He still felt that there might be a last minute change when the opposition might send the remaining Jewish prisoners to Auschwitz prior to settling. Finally, according to Father's plan, the forty-six people from Berg and six from Grini, the other camp in Norway, were sent via the Ski station outside of Oslo to Sweden where they arrived in the afternoon of May 2, 1945. Seven of them, six men and one woman, were stateless and came originally from Germany, Austria and Czechoslovakia. Those with Norwegian citizenship were given new clothes, proper food and pocket money. Those who were stateless refugees were left to their own devices where the circumstances were unacceptable.

When the war ended, only six days later, the seven who were stateless after having spent the war years as Norwegians, were not allowed to return to Norway when the war came to an end. The same pertained to more than 200 other stateless Jews who had also come to Norway during the "in-between war" (the thirties) and later escaped to Sweden.

This situation upset Father. He made sure that the seven got out of the primitive location where they were staying with friends and acquaintances in Sweden. He tried to turn the focus in the direction of these circumstances by placing pressure on the Norwegian authorities in Sweden to allow them to return to Norway now that the war was over. He was trying to get in contact with the Norwegian press through the Swedish foreign department. The most important writer was Einar Skavlan, the editor and head of the Norwegian newspaper *Dagbladet,* who wrote several leading articles about this issue. Father wrote a chronicle in the same major newspaper, where he strongly criticized the Norwegian authorities. He also included the horrible refugee politics which had been pursued during the thirties concerning the refugees, which he now hoped had ended. Among other things, he wrote the following:

Some of the stateless people happened to be in Norway just by chance, when their home country was occupied. They were allowed to remain there, but without permission to work. Only a very few stateless people had been given this permission. Their personal financial situation was poor and some of them were given support from the Swedish state. Was there a fear that these people would become a burden on the Norwegian state if they got involved with special circumstances? That may have been the reason they refused to allow the people the option to come back to Norway once the war was over.

I cannot guess and I also hope that this type of reasoning should have been ignored. During the years before 1940 when Norway opened its doors to a few people, the country also took on a moral obligation towards these persecuted persons, totally unrelated to the expectations they had anticipated upon their arrival. The number of people was small—much too small. Konstad (The Central Passport's leader) took care of that. Those few stateless who were allowed to enter, with the exception of a handful who backed out, thanked Norway with gratitude and have during all these years continued to express the same. Some of them fought for the Norwegian forces.

Several months were to pass before the stateless Jews could return to Norway.

Refugees and the Joint Distribution Committee

One of the most unexpected, yet interesting situations was how Father connected with the Joint Distribution Committee (JDC) when we lived in Sweden. I am not sure exactly how he came across this wonderful organization, but I know it took place around 1944, about a year prior to the end of the war. As mentioned previously, Father had escaped to Sweden with his immediate family at the end of 1942 when he realized the severe danger which was awaiting Norwegian Jews. Around 1944 he was hoping against hope that the war perhaps would end soon.

Just before the end of 1944, Father met Charlie Jordan. The latter held a major position at the American Joint Distribution Committee—also known as the JDC. This was one of the most important organizations Father had heard of since their work reached millions of people suffering during the war. As the light was slowly beginning to show in the distance around the end of 1944—the beginning of 1945, Father started gradually and thereafter frequently to communicate with the JDC. The latter attempted to send a variety of items to numerous camps where prisoners still needed help. By early 1945 the organization was providing necessary help and soon thereafter Father was asked to participate as a middleman, which presumably might simplify their work. Shortly thereafter he became the intermediary between the U.S. and Germany, working very hard to generate and send the material to the people in need.

Father continued in this capacity for at least one year in addition to his other activities. The goal was to send medication and food to the poor refugees who were still waiting at the camps hoping for the end of the war which rumors indicated would be soon. Father finally decided to return to Norway with his family in the middle of 1946.

At the end of 1943 Mother had taken ill and was both hospitalized and separated from us for over a year. During his time in Stockholm Father continued working in the same position at the Jewish Congregation where his responsibilities gradually increased. The likelihood of a positive solution related to the deported Jews became more and more likely.

At the end of every day, Father went to the hospital to see Mother before going home to the rented apartment to check on his two small children. Ruth stayed with the family, but took cleaning jobs with other families to make some pocket money while the children were at school and in play groups.

I have a very strong memory of Father when he returned home one afternoon. I must have been around six. I normally played with all the local kids. I was never allowed to cut my hair and I therefore had long, thick braids. On that day I had heard about groups of gypsies moving along the streets. I was watching these groups of all ages who spoke a foreign language. It must have been unusual for the Swedish children to see such a big group of people, all of whom had dark black hair. This had captivated the local kids who watched them go by. Father asked me what I had done that day, as he always did when he returned home. My answer was ready for him, "I have seen gypsies today. And my friend who lives next door asked me if I was a gypsy because I also have black hair!" Father's reaction was totally neutral but he asked me how I responded. I think I said something like "Of course not. I told her that I have black hair because I am Norwegian, and not blonde like the Swedish kids." This became a family story.

As anticipated, WWII came to an end in May 1945. However, Father's relationship with the JDC was not to end. On the contrary, this was to become an ongoing work connection that would last for many years. When our family returned to Norway in the summer of 1946, the JDC assumed responsibility of all the existing papers and documentation of what had happened in Norway during the war and contemplated how they could help Norway. The material was passed on to the JDC in New York.

For two years father continued to make short interim visits to the JDC in Stockholm. I am convinced that returning to Norway must have been both a relief as well as a difficult time, considering all the changes in everyone's lives.

The War Is Over
Back to Norway

Finally, the war came to an end. The Norwegian Jews who had lived in exile in Sweden waited for freedom. It took three years. Ruth had remained with us until the war was over. She decided to go back to Norway eager to see her family. She did however return when we were back in Oslo in 1946 and stayed with us until both my parents passed away. Leif and I considered her a second mother.

People's reactions vacillated regarding the final result. Some were naturally extremely glad, while others felt a sadness which couldn't be removed. These combined reactions took place for many years. Of course they were returning to Norway now that the war ended and they could walk freely in the streets. Would they be able to remember the past, long before the attack by Germany? Their families, their parents, their children and grandchildren? Life would never be the same. Which friends would they meet? Who would be there? What should they say if they met an old friend but wasn't sure if their parents had survived? The reality was that about 40 percent of the Jews in Norway were no longer there.

The large synagogue in Oslo remained, apparently untouched. What a miracle! But the rabbi and the cantor were no longer present. They had been killed. The members of the congregation had no choice but to rebuild.

The Jewish exiles went looking for their apartments. Knocking on doors saying, "Hello, my name is…. This is my home. I used to live here until I had to escape (or before I was arrested and sent to Germany)."

If the newly-arrived people had been lucky enough to return to their previous homes, they began to assess the premises. Where is the big sofa which sat in the corner? And what about the table and chairs? What happened to the pictures on the walls and the vases in which we always kept flowers?

They needed to contact friends or even strangers to see where they should start looking!

Little by little Father managed to open his store and worked together with his brother Alf who ran a similar business. I often wonder what it felt like starting all over? Immediately after Father returned to the present political situation to see how the Norwegian sources were to deal with the post-war. Many of the refugees who had worked hard to escape to Norway in the mid-30s wanted to remain there. However shortly thereafter it was made clear that now the war was over, and these stateless people were expected to leave to find another country.

The Norwegian government no longer showed interest in helping or supporting the refugees. They felt they had done what was necessary, as the refugees were not Norwegian by birth. The fact that they were still stateless although in Norway, they no longer had permission to remain there. Father felt that this was a humanitarian issue as these people were desperate. He did all he could trying to find a solution.

Father became even more eager to solve this problem. He contacted the JDC and I believe this was the beginning of their close professional relationship which lasted for the rest of his life. Father started attending meetings and conferences in Paris where the JDC initiated possible activities. He also met representatives from the JDC in Stockholm where they continued working together, both sides grateful to help each other.

As I was getting older, I realized that increasingly more and more Americans visited Oslo to see Father which resulted in important work during the next few years. This also gave him an opportunity to meet some exceptionally active people for many years to come. My parents hosted a variety of people from various countries through the years, mostly from the U.S., who were affiliated with the JDC and eventually became close friends. There is no question in my mind that Father's ongoing and long-time relationship with the JDC was the most important development in his life. It allowed him to fully develop and utilize the support and expansion necessary to help suffering people in Europe.

1947
Father's Philosophy—
Personal Unresolved Issues

The papers which Father left behind very seldom included his personal opinions about the activities in which he participated. It was the actual work which kept him busy—not the thoughts surrounding it. In one instance, Father had a very strong emotional reaction. The first time was when the Gestapo's Wilhelm Wagner, Eichmann's emissary in Norway, was sent to court. He was not sentenced to death, but granted twenty years of hard labor in 1947. Father wrote several letters to the public prosecutor about this matter, a case for which the Jews felt extremely fervent. He wrote several letters to the public prosecutor about this case which had seriously upset the Norwegian Jews. Father demanded that the public prosecutor initiate another complaint against Wagner. He referred to a number of additional complaint issues which the public prosecutor had chosen not to include when dealing with this case. Among other issues, Marcus Levin also stated the following:

> The final result has had a very strong depressing effect on me as well as on others—both Jews and non-Jews. The punishment, according to my opinion, is too lenient for such a horrible crime executed by Wagner. The issue for which he has been accused, has resulted in a severe depression as well as confusion.

Father also expressed the following:

> It is impossible to free oneself from the feeling that the judgment is expressing reduced consideration pertaining to a specific group of humans which is the issue here—therefore we ask ourselves whether the court would have arrived at the same result, had the case pertained to another group of Norwegian citizens.

Here he is referring to an article written by Bernhard Goldberg, Father's closest friend. "Are We Jews Still of Less Value?" The article in question was printed in *Dagbladet* in May 1947. The article is still available by request.

Bernhard Goldberg was actively involved studying medicine at the beginning of the war. He signed up as a volunteer with the Norwegian Navy and remained with them until the liberation. He was torpedoed twice and was given the St. Olav's Medal with a Branch of Oak (St. Olav Medaljen med Ekegren) which was the highest medal given to a participant in the Navy during the war. He was the most highly decorated Norwegian Jew. Goldberg had been a very close friend of Leonard Levin, Father's youngest brother, who also was a physician. As mentioned earlier, Leonard was killed in Auschwitz. When Bernhard returned from the Navy after the war, he found that his parents, sister and two brothers had all been killed. Despite his difficulties adjusting to life in liberated Norway, he returned to medical school and completed his degree. Father and Bernhard Goldberg were quite similar in attitude and principles. They were also brothers-in-law, married to two sisters, our mother Rosa Levin and her younger sister Amalia (Makka) Goldberg. During our early years, my brother and I were extremely close to Uncle Bernhard who we considered to be a second father. It was obvious that the two men supported each other during the post-war years. Bernhard Goldberg passed away suddenly in 1958.

There was no response from the public prosecutor pertaining to the documents. In addition, William Wagner's sentence was reduced and he was told to leave Norway in 1952, after only five years in prison. Once again Father would express a certain bitterness related to the treatment which the Norwegian Jews experienced.

At the end of the fifties, Father told my brother Leif that one day he spotted Wilhelm Wagner on the most significant street in Oslo, The Karl Johan, which both then and now is located with a major view of the king's beloved castle. The castle is located only a few minutes from the highly admired and well-known university which has always been the center of Oslo for many, many years.

1945
Returning from the Holocaust

The day people were hoping for, had finally arrived. The rumors of horror were finally confirmed, and suddenly life had changed. The war had come to an end, yes, which indicated bombs, shooting and last but not least, ongoing murders. Time had passed for people to wonder, speak of rumors, and finally learn what had taken place.

In April 1945 Father was one of the few Jews who had continuously participated and had kept apprised of all the suffering horrors he had documented. He had not yet returned from Sweden to his homeland. He immediately went to the Swedish West coast where he had been alerted that very few Norwegian Jews were to be transported home. All together they announced that thirty-five men had survived. Not a single woman survived. The survivors from the concentration camps arrived on one of several white buses. Two Jews, Lieba and Josef Berg, arrived in Helsingborg. Father interviewed them. He also met his old collaborator partner Odd Nansen, who was responsible for the NansenHelp organization and who had been sent to Auschwitz. He was not Jewish but he had been arrested for actively fighting against the Nazis. He told Father when they met that he had written a secret diary while imprisoned. During 1943–44 Nansen had written down what he heard about the horrendous treatment of the Jews through conversations with two survivors from Norway at Sachsen-Hausen, Eugen Kell and Lieba Wolfberg. Sadly enough he also told Father that he hadn't seen his brother, Leonard. Initially the two had spent much time together while imprisoned in Northern Norway prior to both being deported to Germany. He suspected Leonard was no longer alive.

Sometime thereafter Father also interviewed other survivors, including three friends, Samuel Steinmann, Julius Paltiel, and Robert Savosnick. He also wrote the first documented report dealing with the destiny of the Norwegian Jews, writing in a straightforward manner. Father received a stream of letters from friends and relatives of the deported Jews during the war years. Many had heard rumors that their husbands or sons were among the survivors. In most instances Father's replies were negative. Among those who died were Father's brothers Sigurd and Leonard, as well as his sister Leah Steinfeld, who had been deported from Aalesund with her husband and two children, as well as two brothers-in-law.

In retrospect, it is disturbing to note that the Norwegian authorities showed no interest in Father's work at that time or in the tragedy related to the destiny of the Jews.

Return from Auschwitz
Post-war Contact with the
Norwegian Government in London

In 1945 the war was over, but there were many gaps and holes to fill. The enormous and unreal number of humans who had lost their lives was more than anyone could ever imagine. Father continued faster than ever striving to help the survivors. I often think that his need to devote time and energy to help others may have been his only way to continue to live, considering the loss of several close relatives, while he survived.

Father asked the Norwegian government in London whether the few surviving refugees who had come to Norway prior to 1940, could remain in Norway even though the war was over. Of all the refugees who had arrived earlier, very few had survived. Most of them had been deported and killed. Father was deeply disappointed by this and other issues which were connected to the Norwegian official government in exile. Any declaration stating that the Norwegian government would assume responsibility for the Jews who had been deported from Norwegian soil, never arrived. Father's biggest disappointment was when the Norwegian government failed to take on the obligations which other Nordic countries expected would be the responsibility of the Norwegians. The survivors were still stateless after having been the victims of the Gestapo during the war years. In retrospect, I can begin to understand why the government didn't respond. The country had a number of other problems to deal with and the refugees from other countries were not at the top of the list. Father's reaction was not intended as a criticism of the decision, but most probably as a sadness.

In addition to the pain and pressure which took place among these people, there was an issue that needed to be addressed. This was in connection with the destiny of those who had been deported, but had survived. There was a lack of consensus whether they should still be taken care of by the expected assistance in Norway or by the international contingent which would be initiated as soon as the opportunity was available, bringing all back to their respective native countries. But that didn't happen.

Father's letter to the Norwegian government in London consisted of the following request:

> The people who we are dealing with today have no home country to which they can return, unless Norway will open its doors again where they can rest quietly to decide whether to remain in Norway or choose another country if possible.

However, once more London did not respond to this request.

Despite the fact that Norway had allowed the refugees to come to their country in the nineteen thirties and prior to WWII, they no longer wanted any of the refugees to stay. In 1945 when the war was over, the Norwegian government no longer was interested in taking on this burden. In a letter to the Norwegian government in London in September 1945, Father described how relatives and friends of this particular group suffered pain and sadness. Father never heard back from them. He, as a humanitarian, turned in another direction trying to find a solution.

A detailed list of all Norwegian prisoners in Germany's camps and prisons was prepared. It was difficult to find out in which camps the Jews had been located. Once again, some Jews had, for a variety of reasons, been deported in a Western direction after first having been in Auschwitz. In cases like this, their names were listed as prisoners in a variety of different camps. It is quite clear that the overview which the Bernadotte-action had of the Norwegian Jews, had been developed by Marcus Levin. A copy of the list which contained 749 names was prepared by Father.

Father continued his work for the Jewish Congregation in Stockholm for more than a year after the liberation. During this period the full extent of the Jewish catastrophe became evident. Survivors were spread all over Sweden. Most of them were alone and some were stateless. The largest Jewish centers had been attacked. More than three million Polish Jews were killed. Jewish people in the Baltics, White Russia and Ukraine were eliminated. Many surviving Jews were exposed to new attacks when they returned to their homes in Poland and other Eastern European countries. Therefore, many chose to remain in Germany or to move there after the war. Altogether there were more than 200,000 Jews in camps in the British, American and French zones in Germany. They were called Displaced Persons (DPs), refugees without a home.

1946
Displaced Persons

In August 1946 an international conference consisted of members of the United Nation's new organization for refugees, UNRA (United Nations Relief and Rehabilitation Administration), was held in Geneva. Norway offered to receive 600 displaced and lost Jews. This was intended as replacement for the Norwegians Jews who were deported and killed during World War II.

Internal documents from the Main Advisory Group at the Central Passport office in Norway provided the basis for this refugee effort. It was written as follows:

The advisory group recommends that permission to travel be given to the equivalent number of Jews who were deported and killed in German concentration camps; approximately 600.

The condition was that the Norwegian authorities should make a selection among the potential displaced persons. It was assumed that the appropriate workers would present proof of their earlier work experience, with evidence coming from both previous employers as well as labor associations. In addition, each individual person would be subject to a personal examination related to political position and security.

Those chosen were mainly experienced workers and their families. During the selection they were promised work in Norway within three months after their arrival. Among the Jews a Jewish Social Group was initiated in 1947 as part of the Jewish Social Unit in Norway, both in Oslo and Trondheim. The Social Unit often provided significant transfers from the JDC. Father, who at that time had been appointed a representative for this organization and the leader, Joseph Berg was appointed secretary. He had come from Vienna to Norway in 1938 but was deported to Auschwitz in 1942. He survived and returned to Norway after the war.

Looking forward to a new life in Norway

The organization had offices in the former small synagogue in Calmeyergaten 15 where the Jewish Museum in Oslo is now located. The building had previously housed many stateless Jewish families living in various apartments until the war broke out. Most of the families were arrested and deported, never again to return to their homes. A group of several other social workers was hired by the Social Unit to get this plan organized. Only a few weeks prior to the arrival of the first group of displaced persons, Father realized that the newly arrived people should be temporarily housed in a previous German military camp at Halden; a small town just outside of Oslo, where language classes were arranged for them. The Norwegian government offered a weekly contribution of five kroner per adult refugee, a very small amount, even according to the standard of those days.

Some of the stateless and misplaced Jews were also sent to isolated small areas in the country. In the archives belonging to the Jewish Social Unit a letter was found from a lonely newly-arrived Jew who was located in Andalsnes where he had absolutely no one with whom to communicate. The fact that he also couldn't understand Norwegian was a distinct problem. He wrote to Father that if he was not relocated, he would take his own life. Norwegian authorities had difficulties understanding the problems which the refugees were facing. Father did his best to solve this problem, but without success.

Ads were placed in Oslo newspapers trying in vain to find more local housing. Father reported the endless problems finding housing in Oslo to the JDC. I even remember driving in the car with Father on several occasions when he was trying to locate a small apartment for one of the refugees. The poor refugee would do anything, as long as he and his family could live in Oslo where they could meet other Jews, as originally agreed. The housing shortage was worse than ever. Only one year after the first large refugee group arrived, Father once again sent a report to the JDC. He felt that the entire project had been in vain. He wrote among other things: "The office in the Social Department which was given the responsibility for the refugees, has turned out to be so incompetent that the entire plan may become a catastrophe." He noted further that increasingly more responsibility for the refugees had been passed from the Social Department to the Jewish Social Unit, which had inadequate resources.

Most of the refugees wanted to stay in Oslo where there were Jewish institutions and environments. This was a distinct dream for most of them. Many of the refugees complained to Father and the Jewish Social Unit about the circumstances. It was the Social Department's people who were the visible proof of the authorities' presence, and therefore were subject to a variety of problems and frustrations. In this case the issues also had to deal with the refugees suffering from intense trauma and a difficult past. At that time no other country had considered or dealt with important issues like the above-mentioned problems.

In an effort to start solving the problem, Father convinced the JDC to join him in a plan to sponsor twenty houses at Oppsal, outside of Oslo. In 1949 the work made it possible for some of the refugees to live a more normal life, although even here discussions and problems occurred. Some of the inhabitants in the Oppsal area reacted to what was referred to as the *Jewish ghetto* in town. The group which was already in charge of building came up with names like *Jew Town* as well as *House of Sweden* which they passed on to other people. The former Housing Organization is still present today in the area at Ulsrud Hageby.

All together 492 displaced persons came to Norway in 1947 with more arriving during the following years. In 1951 only 208 people remained as most of them left for Israel in 1949. Others managed to get permission to travel to the USA or Canada and many more left Norway during the 1950s.

Father and the Social Unit's work to help the refugees cannot be under-estimated, despite the fact that the first organized Norwegian refugee contribution in history was not as successful as expected. This should have been the responsibility of the Norwegian authorities. They showed good will, but didn't fully understand the extent of the work, nor the mental state of the refugees. Still the people who did remain in Norway contributed greatly to increase the small minority of Jewish people.

1948
The European Children's Camp in Norway

As the leader of the JDC in Norway, Father was also involved with the so-called Children's Camp in Holmestrand in 1948. This organization in Norway went by the name *Europahjelpen* (Help for Europe) which worked together with the International Jewish Aid Organization. Their plan was to help various Jewish families suffering in North Africa. The children were brought to the camp in groups, operated by a woman from Norway named Mathilde Oftedahl. On November 20, 1949 a plane with twenty-eight children on board crashed about thirty minutes prior to landing. Only one of the children, Isaac Allal, survived the tragic accident.

It feels strange for me to remember this terrible incident so many years later. I often visited the children's camp as Father again was the Norwegian representative for the JDC together with a number of other national leaders. I tried to communicate with the children, but they couldn't understand me. I remember they were all wearing blue and white outfits. The round-trip took us about four hours.

Most of all I remember the accident. I am almost certain it was on a Sunday. I was twelve. I had nothing to do that day but was waiting to see a children's Christmas play at a large theater in Oslo later in the afternoon. Father asked me to come to the airport to meet two airplanes scheduled to arrive. He used the opportunity in the car to tell me about the children from North Africa where life was difficult. The purpose was for the kids to be exposed to a more routine way of life and manners prior to continuing on to Israel. A few other official people were waiting at the airport around the middle of the day, some of whom were newspaper representatives. I spent time waiting just like everyone else. I cannot remember when the first plane arrived exactly, but I recall we were waiting for the second plane. We were told that the plane was late but it seemed like a long time—and it was indeed a very long time. No one at the airport had any idea what had delayed the arrival. What I can remember most of all was Father continually pacing back and forth as he obviously was becoming concerned. Three hours passed. Father spoke to a mutual colleague who was on his way out. He offered to give me a ride back to Oslo so I could get to the theater. Father remained at the airport. I still member the name of the play, *A Journey to the Christmas Star.*

When I returned home, Father was there as well. He was very serious and I was afraid to ask any questions. I knew instinctively that the news was bad. It took two or three days to locate the plane. When I came home from school in the afternoon that day Ruth opened the door, and the first thing she said was, "They found the plane." It was clear that a terrible accident had taken place. The telephone was ringing all day; newspaper reporters asking questions, both in Norway

Marcus Levin welcomes Golda Meier, former Prime Minister of Israel,
arriving in Norway to participate in a memorial service concerning the
fatal plane crash and the large number of children and teachers who perished.

as well as in other countries. The next day I was told that only one boy, a little younger than me, had survived.

Father was going to see him in the hospital and asked if I wanted to come. I don't know why, but I went with him. All I remember was I stayed in the back of the room while Father tried to communicate with him in a language I had never heard. The young boy was sitting up in bed. He had scratches on his face, but other than that, he was looking at the people around him. Then Father took me home.

With the benefit of hindsight, I came across something which suddenly appeared in my work on Father's ongoing effort to not leave any stone unturned. In view of this tragedy to take place in a distant and reasonably unknown country as Norway, it is clear that the hardworking and devoted people from a variety of countries around the world were aware of the long-term years of suffering of children and adults. Mutually they did everything to help. Sadly enough another unexpected catastrophe occurred and quickly was exposed to a total disaster which came from nowhere, and could never be restored.

I was a young girl who remembers the horrible event as I have written earlier. It is obviously clear that I never forgot this incidence. It may sound bizarre when I by chance found a picture regarding world news. What I found was that the official organization in Norway organized an emotional and important event out of respect for around thirty youngsters.

When I saw the unexpected article I noticed two people in the picture. The man was clearly my Father who was standing next to Golda Meier, who had made a special trip to Oslo in 1950 when the horror took place.

1938
A Jewish Children's Home in Oslo — Boys and Girls from Vienna

In the late thirties Jews were increasingly more mistreated. Many people tried to leave the country but found it difficult. They were told they would have to surrender their nationality if they left. However, in the summer of 1938 an increasing number of Jewish families were now severely concerned about their children's future. In Vienna arrangements were prepared to allow a small group of children to temporarily leave their country. The program was not intended to last a very long time. Norway limited itself to welcome close to thirty children. Some parents also anticipated that a country so far away from their present situation wouldn't be exposed to the ongoing fighting at home. They thought the Jewish children might enjoy peace in a city far away at least for a short time. However, two years later, in 1940 Germany attacked Denmark and Norway.

Some of the parents requested their children be returned; which left twelve children remaining. A Jewish Children's home was quickly established in Oslo. In November 1942 the staff of the home was alerted that the remaining refugee children, regardless of age, were scheduled to be arrested by the Germans. The director and several devoted people managed to quickly remove all the children from the house in the middle of the night without a moment to spare. Apparently they spent a short time in several houses to avoid arrest. With the help of a few resistance men, the children were transported directly from Norway to neutral Sweden, along with a few other concerned people. When the war was over, the children returned to Norway where they now felt they belonged, knowing that the Germans were gone. Sadly enough none of the missing parents were heard from again for a variety of reasons. The memories of their early years prior to coming to Norway had vanished due to their young ages. They felt they belonged with the kind people in Oslo who had taken care of them. The children were given permission to stay in Norway despite belonging in another country. This process was arranged by the Jewish Congregation and aided by my Father, the JDC, as well as humanitarian Odd Nansen at Nansenhjelpen.

The children remained in Norway and attended school until they reached adulthood and were able to plan their own lives.

1953–1955
Minus Refugees

The next issue dealt with almost impossible problems. The so-called displaced persons in Europe were exposed to the most difficult situations until the middle of the nineteen fifties. The expression *minus refugees* referred to the poor people who still had to remain in refugee camps. Why did they stay once the war was over? The only reason was they had nowhere else to go. They had no home or country to which to return. And, most of all, no one would hire them as workers because they were either sick or incapacitated. The refugees didn't have the type of competence which European or overseas countries looked for, or in some instances they were mentally and physically broken down after their war experiences. Several suffered from serious illnesses such as tuberculosis or polio.

When these people were finally invited to Norway, they were referred to as *minus refugees*. It may perhaps seem strange that even after the first major Norwegian refugee group, with each participant examined and exposed to various complicated circumstances, Father still showed great excitement about the opportunity to participate and help. He communicated with a number of individuals who might be willing to help the newly arrived refugees find something to do. Father was invited to travel with a small group of other interested representatives to various places in Europe. Their goal was to communicate with each person. Language was a problem. Father spoke German and was able to communicate with some of the refugees who could express themselves only in homemade Jewish (Yiddish), going back to their childhood days.

The professional group decided to invite even those people who suffered from medical and psychological problems. They were encouraged to bring along their closest healthy relatives. Once again the JDC recommended a plan to the Norwegian authorities asking them to help the so-called *minus refugees*. In 1952 an agreement was therefore entered into between the Norwegian Social Department and the JDC, including 36 refugees in this category. The JDC paid a per capita sum for each refugee; $1,600 for each sick refugee, and $800 for each healthy family member. In addition, all their transport expenses were covered.

Several refugees in this group arrived in Norway between 1953 and 1955. As far as this work was concerned, both the Norwegian government and Father became true pioneers. Norway was the very first country to receive refugees of this category in a totally organized manner. The number of people was limited, but the work paved the way for other larger and significant nations.

Marcus Levin and colleagues greeting refugees

Circa 1960
Reconstruction in Norway after the War

Father was involved in more than refugee work. With an extensive international network, he received about $90,000 for the construction of a Jewish community hall located next to the Oslo synagogue, courtesy of the Claims Conference. The community hall was officially opened in 1960. This was no doubt a significant contribution to help Jewish life in Norway continue. Father was one of the most central persons in Jewish war—and postwar time in Norway. His interest did not focus specifically on traditional congregational life. He was actually more interested in looking beyond Norway as well, connecting the Jewish minority to the European reality. His style and approach during these periods were occasionally criticized within the Norwegian-Jewish environment, but this did not affect him. His goal was purely to help other Jews.

Compensation for Norwegians

In 1959 Norway entered into an agreement with the federal republic of Germany for compensation to Norwegians who had been killed or forced to tolerate imprisonment. However, the current Norwegian rules placed those with a Jewish background in a unique negative situation.

The reason, they claimed, was that according to the rules, siblings could not inherit from siblings. In a letter from the Jewish federal communities in Norway to the Government's Social Tribulation Committee in 1961, as many as 250 Jews who were killed did not have any relatives who could have asked for restitution. Father, however, had siblings, but in view of the same principal, he could not ask for restitution—two brothers and one sister. However, in a complaint to the committee in reference to prisoners and retribution, Father came across some interesting circumstances related to the specific problems against which the Jews had to fight against both during and after the war.

The Jews in Norway were exposed to German attacks in a totally different manner than other Norwegian citizens. The latent psychological pressure resulted in the Jews feeling totally deprived of peace of mind as compared to other Norwegian citizens. Even without participation by the Norwegian resistance movement, they were exposed to German misbehavior and other inappropriate excessive treatment and handling. They were also terrorized by Norwegian Nazis who were taking advantage of their exposed situation. Several false complaints were submitted to blame the Jews, which was later proven as being totally incorrect. Consequently, the arrested Jews clearly suffered psychological trauma to a much larger degree from which only very few people still have recovered.

If a family member was arrested, this normally meant that the person in question was never to be seen again. The arrest of the Jews in Norway was also treated differently than the arrest of others. The action against the Jews seemed to occur for no reason other than their religion. Arrests were encouraged especially when it seemed that a Jewish family wanted to escape. Many of the resistance people required a large amount of money to help, which perhaps was not unreasonable. However, the degree of the amount seemed to vary from group to group. Many of the Jews who had the opportunity to escape to Sweden had to pay significant amounts of money to save themselves. However, in all fairness, a few generous non-Jewish men made a point of hiding as many people as possible regardless of their inability to pay.

The damage settlement which the Jews were given after the war was not on the same level as other Norwegian citizens. No compensation was rendered for the significant amount of business inventory which disappeared. It was stated that this was not war damage but excessive damage due to too much merchandise.

As with all situations, Father stated his objections whenever he felt something which in his opinion was unfair and should therefore be corrected. It was the significant and principle side of his work which turned out to be the most impressive as the years passed by. His few, yet brief comments regarding dramatic events during the war still indicated that he was strongly affected. Most of all it proved that as a human being he had unlimited empathy and understanding due to the Holocaust catastrophe.

The King of Norway and the Watch

Father was awarded the gold Medal of Honor by His Majesty, King Olav of Norway, in 1962 for his contribution during WWII.

When Father met with the Norwegian Royal Highness at the castle to receive the Gold Medal of Honor, the King expressed interest in the watch which his guest was wearing. Father explained that it was a gift from his friends at the JDC in New York on the occasion of his 60th birthday. This led to an interesting conversation about the nature of the watch.

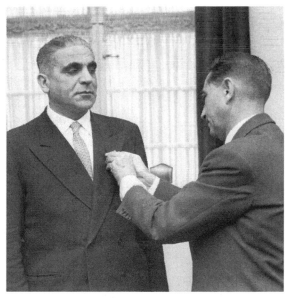

Marcus Levin receiving the Norwegian Medal of Honor

The next day father called the JDC to tell them about the meeting with the King, and his intense interest in the watch. To the best of my recollection it was Charlie Jordan who suggested that Father should contact his Majesty directly, asking if the king would accept an identical watch from the JDC. Father received an immediate response from the Royal Castle expressing the King's great pleasure.

Shortly thereafter a package arrived at Father's personal residence. Father told my brother and me with great pride that when he was invited to return to the Royal Castle's entrance with the gift, he was met by one of the senior guards greeting him in his car saying, "Welcome, Mr. Levin. Go right ahead. You know the way, Sir!"

Marcus and Rosa

1965
Father's Last Years

Father remained JDC's representative in Norway until he passed way in 1965 at 66 years of age.

The general interest in his efforts gradually diminished after his death, even though the Norwegian Refugee Organization honored him in their monthly magazine, *A New Future*. In an article written after his death among other things they wrote the following:

> With the loss of Marcus Levin the Refugee Organization has lost their best advocate. He was still in the midst of helping refugees, both in and outside of Norway. As the chairman of the Jewish Social Tribunal (sosialnemnda) he donated his heart, time and money to help those who were suffering.

Excerpts from some 300 letters were recently made public through archives from the JDC, which dealt with Father's work during the war which he accepted as a major profession in Stockholm. Many of the letters show directly what he wrote to the Swedish foreign department. He was asking for help to get deported refugees returned from concentration camps due to marginal connections with Sweden, through relatives or other Swedish rights. Some of the letters described people questioning whether Marcus Levin had any knowledge as to what had happened to their relatives who had been deported. In addition there are also a few letters containing Father's requests for information pertaining to where his two brothers and one sister with her two children were located.

At the end of the war Father initiated his personal post-mortem search in Auschwitz finding out how long his relatives had managed to stay alive. None of his seven relatives survived. In addition there are documents in the Norwegian archives containing documents showing when Father and his family managed to make it across the border to Sweden.

Our Family Becomes Part of the JDC

The JDC was the organization which inspired Father to continue helping needy people during the war and after, until his last day. The entire Levin family developed a strong relationship with the office in New York which was to continue for several generations. Everyone in the Levin family was impressed by the strong personality of an exceptional, bright and generous man, Mr. Charles Jordan.

My brother Leif and I learned about the people at the JDC early on. We didn't understand exactly how Father got involved, but we learned that this group was based in the United States. Father worked continuously with other countries through their contacts. Both of us remember several representatives for the JDC arriving in Oslo to meet with Father. We didn't know what was involved, only that there were lovely dinners which Mother prepared. Representative after representative came in and out of our house; it was amazing how much pleasure and fulfillment Father experienced when they were present. Mother had lived in the United States for several years before she was married and her English was quite fluent. All of the people were friendly and polite. That's when Leif and I first met Charlie Jordan.

When I was about thirteen or fourteen years old and my brother three years older, we were invited to visit Paris where the European JDC office was located. Charlie and his wife Ellie made arrangements for Leif and me to spend a week in the south of France with two other families. I am not sure if they were working directly with the JDC but I believe they were associated. We had never been to France and had a wonderful experience. We swam in the blue ocean, ate different types of food and had a unique and fantastic week. Once the week was over, we were driven to Paris where the Jordan couple was waiting. Leif stayed in a hotel room by himself which was a great experience and I, being the youngest, stayed at their house. They treated us like close relatives. They showed us around Paris to see famous places, providing us with unforgettable memories.

*JDC Conference in New York, including Marcus Levin (second from right)
and Charlie Jordan (first on left). Photo courtesy of JDC.*

Charlie Jordan was always funny and interested in what we were doing. My
brother in particular remembers that our host was always talking about gadgets;
especially cars. I don't remember any of that, but Leif says there were details in
cars that he had never seen or heard of before. Charlie Jordan must have visited
Norway with Father many times.

It would take me hours to describe how much my entire family cared for him.
One of the stories that Father and my brother clearly remember is the following:

For many Norwegians, Constitution Day on May 17th is even bigger than
Christmas. Norwegians are the only people in Scandinavia who really embrace
national pageantry, and May 17th is the day they pull out all the stops. *Syttende
mai* (May seventh) is always celebrated that specific day. In most places where
there are school children, they march through the main street in town, holding
Norwegian flag, dressed in their very best attire, according to age and class level.
Many of the girls wear beautiful National hand-embroidered dresses (bunads) and
even boys sometimes wear equivalent male costumes.

The most admired and popular march of all marches naturally takes place in
Oslo. Why is this march the most important of all? The march in the capital is
huge; it consists of all school children in town, regardless of their age, and therefore the march lasts for hours. A group of singers of all ages carry Norwegian

flags following a band. The children march up along the royal road entrance leading to the King's castle at the very top. Both sides of the road are covered with thousands of people of all ages watching the children shouting *Hurra* (term of celebration) in response to the music. At the top of the hill the King and the entire royal family wave from the balcony to all the children as they lift their flags with happy sounds. Then the children turn to the right in front of the castle indicating that the march has come to an end. The day will then continue with non-stop fun and games for both children and parents!

Why this long story? On May 17 sometime in the early 1950s Charlie Jordan was in Oslo on business and wanted to experience the special day. My parents attended every May 17 when their children participated, continuing to attend other children's marches even later. On that particular day Leif was with them. Father had explained to Charlie Jordan that this annual event dated back to the very first day of the constitution, on May 17, 1814, when Norway became independent, and had therefore celebrated the same day ever since. Father explained that the entourage of children was a sign to honor the King, together with the other men protecting the country. To the best of my knowledge the choice had been to celebrate the young people of the country instead of celebrating the military.

Charlie Jordan was extremely impressed how young children were prepared to learn how to run the country one day. According to Father, Charlie was so inspired by the ongoing trail of young children walking and singing that he quickly left the side lawn, running to join the youngsters' side-by-side on the walking path for a few minutes. He then returned back to his Norwegian friends and host and hostess with a big, happy smile on his face!

As the children got even closer, they could see the king facing them on the balcony calling back to the youngsters. The poor man must have waved continuously throughout the long day! This was obviously an event to remember! Once the marching band dissolved, the kids joined their parents, looking forward to an entire day of fun.

There are many more episodes which would probably fill this book; however, I am only mentioning the most important events in my life relating to Charlie Jordan and his wife Ellie.

In 1960 I left for the United States for the first time in my life. The plan was for me to spend a year there to work on my English skills. I was greeted by the Jordan couple and taken out for dinner. Charlie told me within a couple of days that although they had no children he had a small group of favorite young people who he considered his special friends. I was included in that group and was told that he would be there whenever I needed any help in the United States. I saw them several times while I was there. My one-year trip resulted in meeting my husband and staying there permanently. The Jordan couple were invited to our wedding in Norway. They sent my husband Martin and me a beautiful, elaborate clock from Switzerland which we have kept ever since.

My mother visited the U.S. several times, but Father did not. Finally he came to the United States for the first time, planning to meet his granddaughters and to visit the JDC. He managed to do all. Just before returning to Norway he was taken seriously ill and spent two weeks in a New York hospital. Charlie Jordan took over from the very first day and made certain that my father got excellent treatment; doing everything possible to simplify his life. Then my parents returned to Norway.

Six months later I was informed that Father was still quite ill. Charlie Jordan was in Norway attending a meeting in Europe and he went to visit Father in the hospital. Mother told me that Charlie was calm and friendly in the hospital room, but walking out, his facial expression changed considerably. It was clear he was very worried. He asked Mother if I was coming. Mother hesitantly said that she was concerned because it was difficult to purchase a plane ticket from the United States as married women didn't have separate access to the bank during those days! The next week Charlie sent a ticket to me and I left for Norway immediately. I was there in time to say goodbye to Father. I will never forget that. Needless to say, Mother returned Charlie's generosity shortly thereafter.

None of us expected Charlie Jordan would leave us so quickly, when he became the victim of a never resolved political murder in Prague. I was visiting in Norway the day it was announced on the radio. I can remember Mother calling Geneva and speaking to Ann Ritt, Charlie Jordan's long-time assistant, asking her if the radio announcement was real. Mother's expression when she started crying scared me. A very long time passed before we absorbed the reality of his horrendous destiny. We will never forget that day. We will always remember him.

1943–1946
Childhood Memories of Sweden

The JDC in New York contacted me in 2016, asking if I could help them in translating some of the documents from Norwegian/Swedish into English. Everyone at the JDC naturally was totally familiar with the story of the escape to Sweden and Father's participation. Beyond that I was told they didn't know many additional details which might be of interest. In view of the large batch of papers which was waiting, they asked if I would clarify the content. We decided I would quickly review each document attempting to summarize each of the important questions verbally to my friend Joanne who took notes, and prepared a condensed translation of the essence of each individual response into English.

In the fall of 2013, approximately 500 documents which had been written to and by Marcus Levin during the early years in exile in Sweden, were finally made available through the archives belonging to the JDC and were labeled as *unknown languages*. For the most part, these documents referred to communications between Jewish refugees and other Jews who had escaped from Norway to Sweden, hoping Father possibly had some knowledge about what had happened to their relatives and friends. They wanted to know what possibly could be done to contact certain people who had not yet arrived. In addition, there were lists of names of Jews who were sent to Germany on another ship called *The Monte Rosa* on November 20, 1942 ahead of *The Donau*. Father's brother Sigurd was on that ship; never to be seen again. Two more ships left as well at the end of January when Nazis and Gestapo celebrated having located all the Jews. Father's sister Leah was sent with her two teenagers on the last ship. Her husband was already sent on a previous ship.

To my surprise I found several personal letters to Father from his brother Alf as he and his wife and daughter lived in another city in Sweden. Two more letters were from my father's Swedish aunts who already knew that our immediate family had made it to safety, as had his brother Alf. The aunts also knew that their sister, father and Alf's mother, Henriette, had lived in Norway with her Norwegian husband, Leib Levin, prior to his passing away. The two aunts went into detail in their letter asking Father if anyone else in the family had made it to Sweden. However, no one else arrived. Seven members of Father's immediate family never made it to freedom.

The letters were all marked as having been written in February 1943. Our immediate family as well as uncle Alf and family arrived between October and November 1942. The two brothers remained close for their entire life having lost their two younger brothers in the Holocaust.

I was more or less in shock when I read these letters, which I had never seen. This had taken place seventy-three years ago! The only pleasant surprise was when I read that the two great-aunts in the letter had sent their best wishes and hugs to "Irene and Leif." Yes, the Irene is me! At that time Leif was about to turn 8 and I was not yet 5. Being the recipient of the letter to Father, which I never even heard of with the hug, finally reached me, and made me cry right on the spot. I suddenly recalled the two elderly aunts, my grandmother's younger sisters. They had lived in Sweden all their lives, as did my grandmother before she moved to Norway to get married. I remember that the two of them also attended my wedding which took place in 1961. I had announced to my fiancé that my entire family expected us to celebrate the day there, since I was going to live in the United States.

Next, I started looking through some of the pictures from my wedding in 1961. I immediately recognized the same two elderly aunts together with Father and his brother Alf celebrating our wedding reception in Oslo. One of the pictures can be found in this book.

Just recently my cousin Mildred, uncle Alf's daughter who was visiting in the United States, showed me a photo. She married a man from Denmark and settled there. Their five children live in Denmark, London, Israel and the United States. The exceptional picture Mildred showed me was of the four generations of her family. One hundred thirty people celebrated her birthday in the mountains of her native Norway. The picture can be found in this book. It was beautiful to see all of them in four rows extending across a large field of green. As I was admiring the picture, Mildred whispered softly to me, "If our fathers hadn't escaped together, our lives would have been dramatically different." When I looked at the picture once more, I echoed her thoughts.

Mildred Guttermann (nee Levin) celebrating with three generations in the mountains of Geilo, Norway, summer 2018

Learning about the Meaning of the Holocaust

Until 1852 Jews were not allowed to settle in Norway. As I mentioned at the very beginning of this story when I introduced my grandfather's early settlement, Henrik Wergeland was the person who worked very hard to change it. He was and is still considered a hero by the Jews. Unfortunately he died in 1845, seven years before his work and devotion were successful.

However, there were Jews living in Sweden and Denmark for several generations. They may have been introduced to the presence of people of other religions which then became acceptable in their countries.

I wonder if most of the Norwegians during the nineteenth and twentieth centuries had little or no knowledge about people who belonged to other religions. Was this the reason why so many so-called *good Norwegians* were willing to help the Nazis eliminate the Jews? Not because they were bad people, but because they had no knowledge as to what was involved? Or was it more?

I never realized that only around 2,000 Jews lived in the country in 1940, if we include the 500 newcomers who arrived only a few years earlier. They were allowed by the Norwegian government to settle in Norway hoping to avoid the anti-Semitism in Central Europe. Except for those few who survived until the war came to the end in 1945, the local Jews as well as the desperate stateless refuges had been annihilated. For those few who were fortunate enough to last that long ended up with other unexpected problems as the stateless refugees had nowhere else to go. The Norwegian government was recovering from five years of German horror and had many other issues to deal with. They informed the refugees that they no longer could remain in Norway.

Growing up Both Norwegian and Jewish

When working on my previous books I realized how difficult the handling of the Jews during the period between 1940 and 1945 had been. When the Germans started attacking both Jews and non-Jews fighting against them, many Norwegian men still remained in the same positions at the main police station, even though it was now run by Nazis and Germans. On one occasion after the end of the war I asked one of the former main members of the resistance group why they had joined the newly reorganized police station in 1940. He answered reluctantly, "At the time, we found that it would be better if the 'good people' were there so we would at least get an idea what was going on." I had no more questions to ask. I couldn't understand what he was referring to. Is it possible that he actually meant what he said? Wasn't that a relatively high price to pay in those days? No one had *any* idea as to what actually was to take place?

As the war came to an end, I learned that many Norwegians had indeed aided, if not supported, the Nazis and soldiers when they were told to arrest and gather the Jews to deport them. I wondered whether those helping them were Norwegian Nazis or because the Nazis actually threatened the average Norwegian to help. Yes, there were risks for both them and their families if they had refused. I can certainly understand it. Fear is not easy. Rumor had it that most of the men who were told to help the Nazis and German soldiers did not dare object. Were they all afraid or were most of them indifferent? At what point does a person avoid danger by giving in? *Don't say no to them. It's not worth it.* Is this what happens when a group of men are concerned and scared, but don't support each other by fighting together? It appears that most of the local men aided the Nazis as a group and no one escaped, but carried on. 500–600 Jewish men were deported to Auschwitz. Only thirty-eight survived. No one knew what really awaited the Jews. They probably didn't consider the possibility of a horrendous catastrophe and killing which eliminated millions of people for no other reason than their religion. But what did they think was going to happen when hundreds of Norwegian Jews and other Jewish refugees innocently were forced to leave the country against their will? The end of this story will include the speech which the Norwegian Prime Minister Stoltenberg delivered in 2012. He apologized to the Jewish Community for the action of the Norwegian police during the occupation His comments were superb with a significant message that hopefully will remind and help people in the future.

Gradually I became familiar with the war horrors, and the indifference which could and should have been avoided; both during 1942 and when the war ended. I memorized what I had heard and the horror remained in my head. It was obvious that Father's helping refugees from Germany escape to safety in the mid-thirties was a constant commitment. However, only a few years later, in 1942, the Norwegian Jews were Germany's next target. From that moment on, Father never stopped helping the victims. His major force and energy remained with him continuously until he passed away in 1965. I doubt that he realized how he

Irene and family in the United States

functioned night and day during his entire life. The JDC was the major support system behind him. He worked on his own, ignoring thoughts that might attempt to slow him down. However, I feel strongly that the many years of association with JDC colleagues must have been the one major link in his life helping people in need as soon as he became acquainted with this organization. Whenever he reached out for support and ability to grow, they continuously reciprocated with mutual respect. Last, but not least there was funding for the post-war peoples' assistance whenever he mentioned potential needs in Norway.

I realized how strong his own personal way of thinking was and how he tried to help as many Jewish people as he could. He spent equally as much time helping his own children. Father always made a point of saying that it was important to marry someone of the same religion, feeling that any successful marriage would be a challenge to acquire. He felt that if you married a person of the same religion, you might hopefully have less problems than if you had to deal with another person's religion in addition to everyday life.

When I was finished with school, starting my life as an adult, I was dating a nice man who was not Jewish. At some point he and I briefly discussed getting married. I mentioned this to my parents. I was quite surprised when mother reacted very strongly saying, "If you marry a man who is not Jewish, I will never speak to you again." I was in shock when I heard this. Father turned to her, raising his voice in anger, "Don't be ridiculous, you don't mean a word you're saying! You would never leave her." After a minute of silence, Father continued. "If you plan to marry someone who is not Jewish, I will use all my energy to talk you out of it. However, if you still marry him, I will spend the rest of my life helping you achieve a happy marriage."

Fortunately, this never became an issue and I made my parents very happy by marrying a very bright, kind, and acceptable Jewish man. The fact that I ended up living in the United States was never discussed. In thinking back, Father never stopped telling me what he felt was right in my life.

Looking Back with Ruth

As time goes by there is more to remember and much to forget. Unfortunately, I grew up relatively quickly once I moved to the United States and became an American. However, I always felt fortunate in that I never forgot the major aspects of my life since then, courtesy of an extensive and wonderful group of relatives in Norway, who never gave up on me and who I never gave up on. My children grew up and by the end of the century they had become independent and we were the proud parents of three daughters and six grandchildren.

For the first twenty-five to thirty years of my marriage I did not speak much about my background in Norway. It was somewhat complicated for me to explain to Americans why I was here, and how long I had been away from Norway. And then came the most common statement with the same expression every time after a relatively quiet intermission, "Oh, are you from Norway? You don't look Norwegian." The person would stare at me and assess the color of my hair. To make it easier for the person to understand why I did not have blond hair and light blue eyes which most Americans thought was the standard with someone from Scandinavia, I lowered my voice and said, "I am a Norwegian Jew." This always resulted with a friendly comment and then the person would say, "Oh, did you suffer at all in Norway during WWII?" For many years I provided a brief response as social or casual conversation did not seem like the right time for an ample explanation.

Around 2003 the last member of my close relatives passed away. This group consisted of my mother and father, and mother's three sisters. Father had several sisters and I had several cousins a few years older than me but I never became particularly close to them. And then, of course, there was Ruth, also known as Ruthin, who had always taken care of me. As I mentioned earlier, Ruth joined my family in her early twenties as a babysitter and a helper performing all types of tasks that mother needed. You can read about her in the early pages of my family's life.

When WWII broke out she escaped with us to Sweden although she wasn't Jewish and under normal circumstances might not be of interest. When my family left with the help of the resistance people, they warned Ruth that it would be best for her to escape as well. They were convinced that if the Germans found her alone after our departure, they would arrest her immediately and pressure her. No doubt her familiarity with all the increasingly serious attacks on local Jews was scary. Consequently, she decided to come with us.

Ruth stayed with our family as long as my parents were alive. She was the one who remained the longest and supported me. When mother passed away, I went to Norway. It was a very difficult time. After my aunts left for the evening, Ruth and I sat alone and talked. I was feeling so bad and couldn't fall asleep. Ruth took my hand and held it until I did. I have no idea how I would have managed to give in to sleep without her.

Aunt Makka, Ruth, and Irene

Every year when I visited Norway, Ruth was the first and the last person I saw. In the middle of 2009, I had a sudden need to speak with her. However Ruth was getting older and had taken ill. I called her a couple times per month and wrote to her all the time. She was the last important woman in my life, and I needed her.

Around the 10th or 15th of January 2013, I got involved in an unusual situation; at least for me. A group of Americans decided that they wanted to compile a book about Norwegian Jews who had managed to survive the Holocaust, and asked me to write a chapter or two for their combined story.

I knew nothing about my family's escape and survival in Sweden. I called Ruth asking her for some details. She told me very little and then paused and said, "many people have tried to interview me about the escape to Sweden." I didn't want to go into too much detail because most of it I had already discussed earlier. However, there was one question that I had never asked anybody before. Why? I don't know. Maybe because I was afraid to ask too many questions. I was always a little shy about bringing up questions concerning the silence which prevailed during my entire childhood from the end of the war until several years later.

"Ruth, I have something specific to ask you." She said nothing, so I continued. "I've had the same dream ever since November 26, 1942 when we escaped. But why did I keep having the same dream so often? I couldn't understand where this story came from because I seem to remember every detail, but no one had ever mentioned it to me." Ruth whispered, "Please continue. What did you dream about?"

I started again by saying,

Please don't laugh at me because I have thought about it for many years. I have a dream about people. I feel that I stood in the darkness next to some big trees on the edge of a small lake. I could only hear my mother speaking to a man who I didn't know. I clearly remember they were arguing. Some light was coming in from above the trees which I assume was the moon. I heard my mother's voice clearly. No, we will not walk across the frozen lake to get to the next part of the forest. I also dreamed that the man was speaking to mother in a loud voice, 'Please trust us.'

I remember the conversation but couldn't place it. I heard mother saying in a strong voice, 'No, the decision is mine. We will not walk across the ice. Ruth has very thin shoes and I am afraid that her feet will get wet if we do. I don't want her to get sick, so I want us to walk around the lake.' It was clearly mother's voice.

I stopped and had anticipated a response from Ruth, but she didn't react. That was the end of my dream.

"Do you think I am silly, or do you have any idea why I told you the story?" Ruth paused for a minute or two, and then said,

Irene, that was not a dream. We were all walking through the forest of Norway on our way to Sweden. You were sleeping in a rucksack belonging to one of the resistance people. Mother was standing at the edge of the lake in the forest. She naturally was afraid of crossing the frozen water and used my shoes as an excuse.

She stopped and I asked, "Who won? Mother or the resistance person?" Ruth answered, "What a question. Of course your mother got her way."

I eventually realized why I had heard Mother's voice speaking to someone, but I couldn't see them. Obviously, I was hidden in the rucksack. Now it makes sense.

January 2012
The Prime Minister of Norway Apologizes to Norwegian Jews

In 2012, Prime Minister Jens Stoltenberg of Norway delivered an announcement intended for all the people in his country. His message expressed that time had come for everyone to apologize to the Norwegian Jews. This was met with enormous response in Norway together with many countries around the world. I was sent a copy of his message in Norwegian, but I also found it in English in a newspaper here in the United States. He started with comments from the highest authority in January 2012,

"Prime Minister Jens Stoltenberg apologizes to the Norwegian Jews for the treatment they suffered during WWII."

NORWAY PARTICIPATED

In one of his first statements Prime Minister Jens Stoltenberg was quoted as follows:

I deeply regret the treatment which the Norwegian Jews experienced during World War II.

The assassination was no doubt the work of the Nazis. But it was the Norwegians who arrested them. It was the Norwegians who drove the cars to get them. And it took place in Norway. I find that today is the time to express our deepest apology for allowing this to take place on the soil of Norway.

Seventy years plus have now passed since the Holocaust took place in Norway. Seven hundred and seventy-two Norwegian Jews and Jewish refugees were arrested and deported during 1942–1945. Only thirty-eight survived.

Without excusing the Nazis of the responsibility, time has come to admit that it was the Norwegian policemen and other Norwegians who participated in the arrests and deportation of the Jews.

Prime Minister Stoltenberg felt that everyone was responsible for fighting the ideas and approaches that resulted in the Holocaust.

> *Now seventy years later it hurts me to say that the ideas which led to the Holocaust are still alive. All over the world we see that individual persons and groups are spreading intolerance and fear. They plant enormous ideologies which lead to antisemitism and hatred against minorities. Driving their attitude out of darkness into the light of knowledge is a responsibility resting on each and all of us.*

It's about time.

The president of the Jewish Congregation in Oslo responded with an appropriate and positive statement based on the apology from the Prime Minister: He makes a division between guilt and responsibility. He continued as follows:

> Jews are still being threatened.
>
> It is good to see that Prime Minister Stoltenberg is responsible for the attitudes and actions to which we are exposed here in Norway. We hope that every member of the country will look at us as their Jews and not a group on the outside. But it is the Nazis alone who are guilty.

He continued to state that the Jews are still a threatened group. Jews are exposed to hatred and discrimination all over the world. As soon as something takes place in the Middle East, the risk for us here in Norway is increased. "Many conspiring theories about Jews circulate around the world today, based on falsehood from the Nazis. There are still groups who encourage murder of Jews and look at us as legitimate goals."

HISTORICAL DESCRIPTION

This is the first time a Norwegian Prime Minister has expressed this type of regret, despite the acknowledgement of Norwegian responsibility which was implicit in the restitution settlement carried out in 1999. At that point the government distributed 450 million kroner as compensation for property and funds which were taken from Norwegian Jews during the war.

This was delivered by the president of the Holocaust Center of Norway.

> Prime Minister Jens Stoltenberg wanted to express his regret "on behalf of all of us."
>
> The expression of regret should have come a long time ago, but it's never too late to acknowledge errors. While I was composing this speech, I noticed that major terms were missing. It's important that they were delivered, as a reinforcement of the financial settlement.

My Philosophy Connected to Prime Minister Stoltenberg

I have read through this important message and the official apology which was delivered in Norway and translated into other languages. This has raised a variety of thoughts.

We know that Norway received its first Constitution on May 17, 1814. There is no doubt that this must have been a challenging and complicated time for the Norwegians to put this into action.

Hopefully, the delivery by Prime Minister Stoltenberg in 2012 was successful in opening the eyes and ears not only of the people in Norway, but as he says, to people all over the world who are suffering because of the nature of their religion and beliefs.

We all have the responsibility of sharing these thoughts and then moving forward. I have been told that Stoltenberg at the end of his well-known speech in 2012, made a point of encouraging not only citizens of Norway, but also people in other countries to focus on learning about other people's religions, allowing them to learn about yours. This will hopefully open the doors for understanding different ways of living peacefully.

THANK YOU, MR. STOLTENBERG.

Afterword

My parents were extremely careful to shield both my brother and me from learning about the horror of the war. When peace finally arrived in 1945, we moved back to Norway. My parents worked very hard not to dwell on the tragedy and instead of answering questions they remained silent—very silent, for many years. When the time came, we learned slowly, step by step. I discovered that many Norwegian Jews had been killed by the Germans, never to be seen again. Many relatives were missing. That is all I heard.

The years went by, and I moved to the United States, married an American, and became a Norwegian/American Jew. We worked hard bringing up our three children, teaching what we thought of as common sense and giving them a good education. We then told our children what religion we practiced and also provided information about other religions.

I didn't speak about the Holocaust, as the subject never came up. Occasionally people would ask me questions, wondering what life was like during the war years. My response was brief as I tried to avoid becoming involved in a lengthy conversation about the Holocaust, which I still had difficulty understanding myself.

Over the years, I learned more about what had taken place in Norway, that while the population of Norwegian Jews was relatively small, the percentage of Norwegian Jews killed in the Holocaust was the highest in all of Europe. And I realized that most Americans knew little or nothing about the circumstances of Norwegian Jews; some knew about Denmark and Sweden but most had no knowledge of or interest in Norway.

Finally I have had the experience to learn more about Norway and World War II. At this time of my life I felt that looking back had given me an opportunity to retain the memories of my family and the country where I was born. As I am getting older, very few members of my parents' generation are still alive. I am grateful that I have been given the opportunity to pass on images and stories of my relatives to my children and grandchildren.

When I received the document from my brother and his friend Bjarte Bruland I was amazed to read of my father's activities during the war. Once I started reading the initial story reinforcing all the details of Father's achievements, I couldn't stop. Of course, I remembered them. Day after day, night after night I had an enormous need to put together all of Father's activities; his energy and the need to help people who were afraid of constant rumors that the Jews were to be annihilated.

Slowly, yet steadily, I remembered and thought about all the events that I hadn't focused on for a long time. I just kept on writing. Gradually I remembered the events in which my father was involved helping stateless refugees. I used to drive around Oslo with Father as he desperately tried to find small, inexpensive housing in a city that was filled to capacity.

By the end of October 2018 I had completed my story about Father's life as a humanitarian. The next morning I felt good waking up. Finally the book was done.

I received a telephone call from a close friend that morning, someone who was born in Norway just like me. "Irene," she said, "I don't know how to tell you this. But I have no choice." Her voice dropped and she continued in a controlled manner. "A horrendous tragedy has taken place at The Tree of Life Synagogue in Pittsburgh. Eleven people were massacred and six wounded. A gunman is believed to be responsible for the deadliest attack on Jews in US history."

This couldn't be. Not now. I received calls from several of my friends, including not only my Jewish friends but also several of my non-Jewish friends, all of whom expressed their sadness. I spoke for only a few minutes and stopped. Several voices within me started to argue. "What do you think now, Irene, will it be ok? How?" I stayed by the telephone. Nothing good could be heard. Horror after horror. What about the book about my father and all the people he had worked with? What about the significant honorary Medal of Merit awarded to him by the King of Norway for helping the suffering Jews throughout all of Europe before and after World War II? I had hoped that this time of my life would have a positive future waiting.

The next day a non-Jewish friend called, virtually in tears. "Why? How can people think like that?" She told me she had grown up in a neighborhood with mostly Jewish families and therefore she was familiar with their style of celebrating each Jewish annual event and felt quite comfortable in the environment. She told me that when she was engaged to be married, she had a casual conversation with her fiancé's father about Jews and marriage. The father said, "Please stay away from Jewish people. They are bad news!" Having had the opposite experience, she said "Sir, do you know any Jews?" His answer was negative. She lowered her voice and whispered "If you don't know any, how can you say they are bad?"

I know that it will take a long time for all the people of the world to learn how to respect and value each other. It will take time to end bigotry and persecution based on religion, ethnicity, and other factors despite the awful examples of the Holocaust and other genocides of the past. It is my hope that my three books on the Holocaust and Norway, including this volume, will contribute to such efforts. We must never forget the terrible things that happened during the Holocaust, but we must also remember the people who fought against Hitler, whether on the battlefields or through humanitarian efforts like those of my father.

We must start by educating our children as early as possible in schools and at home both about history and about the value of every human life. If they are exposed to common sense and education, there may be an opportunity to repair the world. I intend to continue to do my part.

Irene Levin Berman

About the Author

Irene Levin Berman was born, raised, and educated in Norway, after which she moved to the United States as a young bride. Her first recollection of life back to 1942 was how, as a child, she had to escape with her family to Sweden, a neutral country. Germany had invaded Norway and the persecution of the 2,000 Norwegian Jews had started; Seven hundred and seventy-one persons were deported and annihilated by the Germans, including seven members of her father's family.

Irene's first book, *"We Are Going to Pick Potatoes": Norway and the Holocaust, the Untold Story,* is a narrative of that journey back in time. The book was suggested and supported by The Norwegian Resistance Museum. Irene examines the label of being a Holocaust survivor with the subsequent resulting introspection. Irene's strong dual identity as a Norwegian and a Jew forces her to explore all the open doors previously closed.

The book was well received in Norway, and when she translated the book into English it found a "home" immediately. Irene found large groups of U.S. readers who were totally uninformed about the Holocaust in Norway. She had the pleasure of traveling around the country speaking to people of many different nationalities, in particular among Norwegian Americans.

Irene's second book, *Norway Wasn't Too Small: A Fact-Based Novel about Darkness and Survival* follows the fate of two Jewish families during the Holocaust in Norway. One survives by escaping to neutral Sweden while the other, despite fierce effort, eventually is consumed by their German oppressors.